The Sign of the Cross

St. Francis de Sales

The Sign of the Cross

The Fifteen Most Powerful Words
in the English Language

Edited and translated
by Christopher O. Blum

SOPHIA INSTITUTE PRESS
Manchester, New Hampshire

The Sign of the Cross: The Fifteen Most Powerful Words in the English Language is a new translation of *Defense de l'Estendart de la Sainte Croix, from Oeuvres de St. François de Sales, édition complète, tome deuxième* (Annecy: Niérat, 1892) and includes a new foreword by Christopher Check and a biographical note written by the staff of Sophia Institute Press that was originally published in St. Francis de Sales's *Thy Will Be Done* (Sophia Institute Press, 1995).

Copyright © 2013 Sophia Institute Press

Printed in the United States of America

Cover design by Carolyn McKinney

On the cover: Wooden Cross with Design (8898867)
© iStockphoto.com/Jason Deines.

Sophia Institute Press
Box 5284, Manchester, NH 03108
1-800-888-9344

www.SophiaInstitute.com

Sophia Institute Press® is a registered trademark of Sophia Institute.

Library of Congress Cataloging-in-Publication Data
Francis, de Sales, Saint, 1567-1622.
   [Défense de l'estendart de la Sainte Croix. English]
   The sign of the cross : the fifteen most powerful words in the English
   language / translated and edited by Christopher O. Blum.
      pages cm
   ISBN 978-1-933184-97-5 (alk. paper)
   1. Cross, Sign of the. I. Blum, Christopher Olaf, 1969- editor of
   compilation. II. Title.
BV197.S5F7313 2013
242'.72—dc23

                                                    2013011705

9th printing

Contents

Foreword

Catholics who recognize St. Francis de Sales doubtless know, or at least know of, his masterpiece of spiritual direction, *Introduction to the Devout Life*. Offering a path to sanctity later proclaimed by holy men and women from the Little Flower to Josemaría Escrivá, St. Francis showed the common man of the Counter-Reformation that his everyday life was not only a gift from God, but also one that he could return to the Divine Giver. In labor and rest, in toil and triumph, in sorrow and joy, the common man could work out his salvation and give glory and honor to God. The business of holiness, he insisted, was not the special preserve of ordained priests and consecrated religious. Every Christian has a role to play in the economy of salvation, a role great or small depending not on the world's opinion of the grandeur of the undertaking but on something considerably more sublime: the amount of love of God we bring to all that we do.

Three centuries later, in one of the few works that merit mention in the same breath as *Introduction to the Devout Life*, Father Edward Leen devoted a chapter of his *In the Likeness of Christ* to this very truth. The secret of life, Leen teaches, is less of a mystery than we make of it. Leave to God the ends, Father Leen counsels. Instead, attend to your motives: "Let all your actions be done out of love of Jesus Christ."

Father Leen had before him the example of the freshly ordained St. Francis de Sales.

More than a decade before he penned the *Introduction to Devout Life*, St. Francis de Sales's Christian heart—forged in the arsenal of rigorous self-denial and intense study—was tested on the best kind of proving grounds, one where human savagery and holy opportunity collided: Le Chablais, 1594–1598. There, in the words of his biographer, André Ravier, S.J., we encounter not Francis de Sales "the gentle pastor watching over tender sheep and lambs in the midst of meadow flowers," but instead, Francis de Sales the warrior engaged in "missionary combat."

In the sixteenth century, the Chablais was a province in the Duchy of Savoy. Placed by God at the bloody crossroads of France, Italy, and Switzerland, the province was a battleground in the wars spawned by the heresies of that most unpleasant of religious rebels, or "stinker," as St. Francis called him in an unguarded moment, John Calvin. The iconoclasts of Geneva rolled through the once bucolic region of the Chablais, leaving behind political turmoil, hundreds of desecrated churches, and a mere remnant—perhaps no more than a hundred among twenty-five thousand—of terrified and persecuted Catholics holding out hope for a return of the Roman liturgy, the sacraments of the Church, and the joy of Catholic life.

The man who restored the Faith to the Chablais was Francis de Sales. Two years into his priesthood he volunteered for the task. Armed with a Bible and few texts of Bellarmine, and joined only by his cousin, Canon Louis de Sales, Francis left his chapter in Annecy and ventured north.

Belloc's high praise of Thomas More—that in the end he acted alone—applies no less to Francis de Sales in the Chablais. Indeed, the English martyr of not-too-distant memory may well have been an inspiration to Francis, who, save the fraternity of his cousin, found himself altogether abandoned in his effort. Most painful was the resistance from his own father, the Lord of Boisy, who made every effort to discourage his son and refused to give him the least sum to support his venture. "Father, if I did not desire the responsibility," said Francis "why should I put on the cassock?" On the morning of his departure for the Chablais, September 14, the feast of the Exaltation of the Holy Cross, Francis's father would not even bid his son farewell.

On the edge of the Chablais, the fortress of the Baron d'Hermance, a nobleman loyal to Rome, served as a beachhead. Each day, Francis and Louis walked the ten miles into the region's capital city, Thonon. There they preached the Catholic Faith to those who would hear. At the end of the day they walked home. To stay overnight in Thonon would have put their lives in danger, and Francis over the next four years would suffer assassination attempts, attacks by wolves, and the privations of winter. The saint's unshod feet left bloody footprints in the snow.

More discouraging than physical suffering was the apparent failure of the mission. A year passed, and then another, and then another, and still Francis had but a few converts to show for his efforts. In his correspondence Francis describes preaching Advent sermons to "four or five," a number that our Internet-burdened age would judge inefficient, to say the least.

Did St. Francis de Sales yield? Never for a moment.

To the Catholic remnant he brought the sacraments they had so long desired. He slid his tracts defending the

Faith under the doors of Thonon's citizens, and he treated the city's ranking Calvinist clergy with abundant measures of insight, wit, patience, and good humor. When Louis showed signs of losing hope, Francis smiled and assured him that they had planted so much seed that the harvest would not be far off. In the fourth year, like ears of wheat, the converts came, at first by ones and twos — a laborer here and a prominent Calvinist theologian there. Before long Francis's field was flourishing with souls, thousands, brought back to holy Mother Church. As he later described it, "the vines were exhaling their perfume." The young priest had brought love to all that he did. He had left the results to God. And God had delivered.

The conversion of the Chablais is one of the great stories of Catholic apologetics, not so much for numbers, staggering as they were, but more for exhibiting the truth that apostolic work absent an interior life focused on Jesus Christ will not bear fruit. Again and again, in a work no man who is serious about apostolic work should fail to read and reread, *Soul of the Apostolate*, Dom Chautard offers to us the example of Francis de Sales to drive home his point:

In the Chablais district of the Alps, every effort of orthodox Christianity fell through, until the appearance of St. Francis de Sales upon the scene. On his arrival, the Protestant leaders made ready for a fight to the death. They desired nothing less than the life of the Bishop of Geneva. But he appeared among them full of gentleness and humility. He showed himself to be a man whose ego had become so subdued and effaced that the love of God and of other men possessed him almost entirely. History teaches us the almost incredibly rapid results of his apostolate.

It is St. Francis de Sales's heroic mission in the Chablais that has given us the jewel of Catholic apologetics you now hold. St. Francis's *Defense de la saincte Croix de nostre Sauveur Jesus Christ* saw publication in 1600, that is, after the mission to the Chablais, but it finds its origins in a controversy that took place three years earlier. As his mission was gaining steam, and souls, Francis staged a public celebration, the Forty Hours devotion at Annemasse. The two days of festivities included public conferences and religious ceremonies, but also popular songs and the firing of guns. The centerpiece of the celebration was a large cross facing Geneva and erected on the site of a ruined Calvary, desecrated by Calvinists years before. Francis placed around the cross large placards on which was written a Catholic defense of the Holy Cross, its power and proper veneration.

Geneva's theologians read the broadsheets, and one of them, Antoine de la Faye, wrote in reply his *Brief Treatise Concerning the Virtue of the Cross and the Manner of Honoring It*. To this work of literary iconoclasm, Francis would later respond with this book, in fact, four books, of which this is the third, treating the Sign of the Cross. Book 1 deals with relics of the True Cross, book 2 defends images of the Cross, and book 4 explains what it means to honor and venerate holy things.

The reader will not fail to be struck by the relevance of this work in our own age. Crucifixes to be sure, but even bare crosses, are conspicuous by their absence in America's Evangelical churches, and the act of making the Sign of the Cross is regarded by many non-Catholics as superstition at best.

St. Francis gives us a guide and a method to take up the defense of the Cross and the sign we make in its honor. He gives us also a note-perfect example of Catholic apologetics, especially those directed toward our separated brethren. Embodying the zeal of youth and the wisdom of age, the work appeals to the unbroken line of Tradition: from the Fathers, to the Apostles, to our Lord Himself. The treatise reflects the precision of Francis's thought honed in the schools of Paris and Padua. Above all, it is suffused with the love of God, the virtue without which apologetic work will bear no fruit.

Christopher Check
San Diego, California
Feast of St. Francis de Sales
January 24, 2013

The Sign of the Cross

Chapter 1

What Is the Sign of the Cross?

The Sign of the Cross is a Christian ceremony that repre-sents the Passion of our Lord by tracing the shape of the Cross with a simple motion.

It is a ceremony, I say, and here is what is meant by that term. A skillful manager assigns to each of his sub-ordinates his proper task, making all of them useful, not only those who are vigorous and energetic, but also those who are less so. Similarly, the virtue of religion, hav-ing for its proper and natural work to render to God the honor that is His due, draws up each of our virtuous ac-tions into its own work by directing them all to the honor of God. Religion makes use of faith, constancy, and tem-perance for the good deeds of testimony, martyrdom, and fasting. These actions are already virtuous and good in themselves; religion merely directs them to its particular intention, which is to give honor to God. Yet not only does religion make use of actions that are in themselves

3

good and useful; it also employs actions that are indifferent or even entirely useless. In this regard the virtue of religion is like that good man in the Gospel (Matt. 20:6–7) who hires the lazy and those for whom others had found no use to work in his vineyard.

Indifferent actions would remain useless if religion did not employ them, but once put to work by it, they become noble, useful, and holy, and henceforth capable of earning their daily wage. This right of ennobling actions which if left to themselves would be only common and indifferent belongs to religion, the princess of the virtues. It is a sign of her sovereignty. It is religion alone that makes use of such actions, which are — and are properly called — ceremonies as soon as they enter into her service. Truly, inasmuch as the whole man with all of his actions and belongings ought to give honor to God, and inasmuch as he is composed of soul and body, interior and exterior, and in the exterior there are indifferent actions, it is no wonder that religion — having the duty to summon man to pay this tribute — demands and receives in payment exterior actions, indifferent and bodily though they be.

Let us consider the world at its birth. Abel and Cain made their offerings (Gen. 4:3–4). What virtue called upon them to make these offerings if not religion? A little while later, the world came forth from the ark as from its cradle, and without a moment's delay an altar was arranged and several animals were immolated upon it in a holocaust whose sweet odor was received by God (Gen. 8:18–21). In train there followed the sacrifices of Abraham (Gen. 12:8; 13:18; 22:13), Melchizedek (14:18), Isaac (26:25), Jacob (28:18; 33:20; 35:14), and the change and washing of the clothes associated with it (35:2–3). The greater part of the Law of Moses was taken up with ceremonies. Let us now come to the Gospel. How many ceremonies do we see there in our sacraments (Luke 22; John 3), in the healing of the blind (Mark 8), the raising of the dead (John 11:35–44), and the washing of the Apostles' feet (John 13:4–5)? The Evangelical[1] will say that in these things God did what He pleased and that no consequences for our practice can be inferred from them. Yet here is St. John baptizing (Mark 1:4), and St. Paul having his hair cut in accord with a vow (Acts 18:18) and then praying on his knees with the church in Miletus (Acts 20:36). All of these actions would have

---

[1] Each of the eight times in this work that the name *Huguenot* appears to signify the "Reformed" or Protestant Christians of Switzerland, the English term *Evangelical* will be used in its place in order to accentuate the enduring relevance of St. Francis's treatise. — Ed.

been sterile and fruitless in themselves, but employed in the work of religion they became honorable and efficacious ceremonies.

Now here is what I have to say: the Sign of the Cross of itself has neither strength, nor power, nor any quality that merits honor, and, furthermore, I confess that "God does not work by figures or characters alone," as the author of the treatise[2] says, and that "in natural things the power proceeds from the essence and quality of the thing, while in supernatural things God works by a miraculous power that is not attached either to signs or to figures." But I also know that God, in making use of His miraculous power, very often employs signs, ceremonies, figures, and characters, without attaching His power to those things. Moses touching the rock with his staff (Exod. 17:6, Num. 20:11), Elisha striking the water with Elijah's coat (2 Kings 2:14), the sick having recourse to St. Peter's shadow (Acts 5:15), to St. Paul's handkerchiefs (Acts 19:12), or to the robe of our Lord (Matt. 14:36), and the Apostles anointing the sick with oil (Mark 6:13): what

[2] "The author of the treatise" refers to Antoine de la Faye, a member of the Company of Pastors of Geneva, who had written a *Brief Treatise Concerning the Virtue of the Cross and the Manner of Honoring It* in opposition to St. Francis's use of the Cross in his missionary labors in the Chablais. — Ed.

were these other than pure ceremonies, which had no natural power and were nevertheless employed unto miraculous ends? Is it necessary for us to say that the power of God was tied down and bound to these ceremonies? On the contrary, it would be more fitting to say that the power of God, by making use of so many different signs and ceremonies, shows that it is not bound to any one of them alone.

Five points have thus far been made. First, the Sign of the Cross is a ceremony. In its natural quality a cross-like motion has nothing in it that is either good or evil, praiseworthy or blameworthy. How many times is such a motion made by weavers, painters, tailors, and others, whom nobody honors or troubles for it? It is the same with the cross-like shapes and figures that we see in everyday images, windows, and buildings: these crosses are not directed to the honor of God or to any religious use. Yet when this sign is employed so as to give honor to God, even though it be indifferent in itself, it becomes a holy ceremony, one that God uses to many good ends.

Second, this ceremony is Christian. The Cross, together with all that it represents, is folly to the pagans and a scandal to the Jews. Under the Old Law and under the law of nature, the death of the Messiah was heralded in different ways, but these signs were only shadows and confused, obscure marks compared with those we now use, and, moreover, they were not the ordinary ceremonies of the Old Law. The pagans and other infidels have also sometimes made use of this sign, but as something borrowed, as a sign not of their religion but of ours, and in this way the traitor himself confesses that the Sign of the Cross is a mark of Christianity.

Third, this ceremony represents the Passion. In truth, this is its first and chief end—that upon which all the others depend and which serves to differentiate it from several other Christian ceremonies that serve to represent other mysteries.

Fourth, it represents the Passion by making a simple motion, which is what differentiates the Sign of the Cross from the Eucharist. For the Eucharist represents the Passion by the perfect identity of the one who is offered in it and the one who was offered on the Cross, which is none other than the same Jesus Christ. The Sign of the Cross, however, represents the Passion by a simple motion that reproduces the form and shape of the Crucifixion.

Fifth, the Sign of the Cross consists in a motion, which is what differentiates it from permanent signs, engraved or marked out in enduring materials.

As a rule, the Sign of the Cross is made in the following way. It is made with the right hand, which, as Justin

What Is the Sign of the Cross?

Martyr says, is esteemed the more worthy of the two. It is made either with three fingers, in order to signify the Blessed Trinity, or five, in order to signify the Savior's five wounds; and although it does not much matter whether one makes the Sign of the Cross with more or fewer fingers, still one may wish to conform to the common practice of Catholics in order not to seem to agree with certain heretics, such as the Jacobites and the Armenians, who each make it with one finger alone, the former in denial of the Trinity and the latter in denial of the two natures of Christ.

The Christian first lifts his hand toward his head while saying, "In the name of the Father," in order to show that the Father is the first person of the Blessed Trinity and the principle and origin of the others. Then, he moves his hand downward toward the stomach while saying, "and of the Son," in order to show that the Son proceeds from the Father, who sent Him here below into the Virgin's womb. Finally, he pulls his hand across from the left shoulder to the right while saying, "and of the Holy Spirit," in order to show that the Holy Spirit, being the third person of the Blessed Trinity, proceeds from the Father and from the Son and is Their bond of love and charity, and that it is by His grace that we enjoy the effects of the Passion.

The Sign of the Cross

When making the Sign of the Cross, therefore, we confess three great mysteries: the Trinity, the Passion, and the remission of sins, by which we are moved from the left, the hand of the curse, to the right, the hand of blessing.

Chapter 2

A Public Profession of Faith

"We are not unaware," says the author of the treatise, "that several of the Fathers spoke of the Sign of the Cross and of its power, but that was neither with the same intention nor for the same end that it is spoken of today, for they made use of it as a public profession of their Christianity, or as a confession of it either in public or in private. For when the persecutions were widespread and severe, the Christians—not wanting to declare themselves except to their brother Christians—recognized one another by this sign when they crossed themselves; it was a testimony that they belonged to the same Christian religion.

"Moreover, while the pagans mocked the Cross of Jesus Christ and said that it was shame and folly to believe and to hope in one who had been crucified and had died, the Christians, to the contrary, knowing that all our glory lies only in the Cross of Jesus Christ, and that it is the great power and wisdom of God to the salvation of all believers, wanted to show that they were not ashamed of it and made this sign openly in order to say that they were knights who had taken the Cross, that is, disciples of Jesus Christ. In this regard, we should recall what Chrysostom said in his second homily on the epistle to the Romans: 'If someone asks you, "Do you worship one who was crucified?", have no shame and do not lower your eyes to the ground, but instead glory and rejoice in making this confession with your chin raised and your eyes looking straight ahead.' And also St. Augustine, who said: 'To the wise of this world who assail us about the Cross of Christ and say, "What sort of sense is there in worshipping a crucified God?", we respond, "We lack your good sense, for we have no shame in Jesus Christ or in His Cross, and we make it on our forehead, the very seat of modesty. We make it there, in the place where shame appears, in order that it may be clear that we have no shame."'"

The author of the treatise said all of this without pausing to take a breath. Then, elsewhere, in response to eleven passages from the Fathers urged against the Reform, he said the following:

The fourteenth passage is taken from a treatise on St. John, which says: "If we are Christians, we are

attached to Jesus Christ and we carry on our foreheads the mark of the one whom we do not blush
to carry in our hearts, whose mark is his very humility." To this testimony, we would join, for the
sake of brevity, all of the following ones, which are
ten in number, because almost all of them report
that Christians signed themselves on their foreheads. We recognize, therefore, that this custom of
signing oneself on the forehead was introduced in
antiquity — by whom and how it does not matter."
And later he writes: "It has been explained above
what the ancients understood by this sign: that is,
an external testimony to the Christian faith."

Doubtless this confession from my adversary releases
me from the obligation of proving anything further about
this point. But since he wrote these truths in spite of himself, he has watered them down as much as he could.

"Several of the Fathers," he said, "spoke of the Sign
of the Cross." I would ask him to name for me those who
did not speak of it, for he will find few topics outside the
Creed itself to which the Fathers testify as universally and
unanimously as the Sign of the Cross. Why, then, should
he have spoken of "several," as if it were a question of two
or three of them?

The Sign of the Cross

The author of the treatise says that the intention of the Fathers was not the same as it is today, but if he means by that the intention of Catholics, I will help him to see that the contrary is as plain as daylight.

If, however, what he means is the intention imputed to Catholics by the Protestant ministers, as if we were guilty of attributing to the sign what is proper only to the Crucified Himself, I confess that this is not at all what the Fathers thought and that to say that they did is a malicious prevarication.

He says that the ancients made this sign so that they would be known only to their brother Christians. Truly, this is a claim I cannot believe, for what would be the use of making the Sign of the Cross for the sake of remaining hidden from one's enemies? Moreover, to the contrary, he admits a little later that the pagans mocked the Cross and that their common reproach of the Christians referred to it, while the Christians showed that they were not ashamed of it by making the sign openly. Let us set these two arguments next to one another: the Christians made the Sign of the Cross so that they would be known only to their brother Christians; the Christians made the Sign of the Cross openly to show that they were not at all ashamed of Jesus Christ. It is certain that Tertullian, Justin Martyr, and Minutius Felix all testify that the Sign of the Cross was no secret profession of faith and that the pagans knew it well.

He recognizes that the custom of crossing oneself began in ancient times. He speaks in particular of the time of St. Augustine, whom Calvin himself saw as reliable and credited with having changed no earlier doctrines. The author of the treatise even admits that it was only in the time of St. Gregory the Great that Christian eyes began to see the divine service less clearly. From which admissions, I argue thus: no changes in doctrine had been made at the time of St. Augustine; but, in the time of St. Augustine, the Sign of the Cross was commonly made. The doctrine of making the Sign of the Cross, therefore, is pure and apostolic.

He politely declares that it is not known either "by whom or how" this custom of crossing oneself was introduced of old. To this I reply, with St. Augustine, "What is held by the universal Church, and what was not instituted by councils but has always been observed, is most properly believed not to have been given by any authority other than the apostolic one." And I reply with St. Leo that "it must not be doubted that everything that is received in the Church as a custom of devotion comes from apostolic tradition and the teaching of the Holy Spirit." This is the rule by which the Fathers judged ecclesiastical customs, according to which the Sign of the Cross, which has always been practiced by the Church, and comes from no one knows where, should be referred to apostolic institution.

Chapter 3

The Use of the Sign of the Cross in the Church of the Fathers

The Sign of the Cross can be made to testify to belief in the Crucified and thus be a profession of faith or to show that one hopes in and places one's confidence in the same Savior, in which case it is a means of invoking God's assistance in virtue of the Passion of His Son.

My opponent wants to believe that antiquity made use of the Sign of the Cross only for the first end. On the contrary, it was almost never used for this end alone. Rather, its ordinary use was as a plea for God's help. St. Jerome, writing to his spiritual daughter, said: "With every work, with all of your comings and goings, may your hand make the Sign of the Cross." St. Ephraim said: "Whether you sleep or wake, travel or work, eat or drink, sail on the sea or cross a river, cover yourself with this breastplate, clothe and encircle your limbs with the saving sign, and evils will not meet you." And Tertullian: "At every change of place and movement, every going out and coming in, when dressing, when putting on shoes, at the bath, at the table, when carrying a lamp, upon entering a room, and in every action that life requires, we touch our forehead with the Sign of the Cross." "Make this sign," St. Cyril said, "eating, drinking, sitting, standing, going outside, walking, in sum: in all of your affairs." And, elsewhere, "Have therefore no shame of confessing the crucifix, but with confidence let us impress the Sign of the Cross with our fingers upon our forehead, and may the Sign of the Cross be made in all things, eating, drinking, coming in, going out, before sleep, sitting, standing, doing, and remaining idle. For it is a great defense, which for the sake of the poor is given away freely, and for the sake of the weak is made without difficulty, this grace being from God, as the sign of the faithful and to bring fear to the devils." St. John Chrysostom: "The Cross shines everywhere, in places inhabited and uninhabited." St. Ambrose: "All of our works should be done with the Sign of the Cross."

Can such a universal usage of the holy sign be reduced to the profession of faith alone? In every work, rising in the morning, retiring in the evening, in the darkness of the night, and in uninhabited places: to what end would one make this profession of faith where no one could see it? Yet there is more: these Fathers who so strongly recommended the use of this sign never gave as their reason the profession of faith alone without also mentioning the defense and protection that we can receive from it as a breastplate and shield in our trials.

Who does not know that prayer is the general and universal tool of Christians, proper to all of our affairs and works, for every encounter and all of the actions of our life? The Sign of the Cross, then, is nothing other than a brief and lively exterior prayer by which God is invoked, and, as a result, it is proper for all of our doings and plans. Now, that I might be brief, I will content myself with noting only the most significant of its uses: in blessings, consecrations, and sacraments, to chase off demons, to protect oneself against their assaults, and to accomplish other miracles.

Chapter 4

The Legitimate Use of
Ceremonies of Benediction

When he prayed for Lazarus (John 11:41), for His glorification by the Father (John 17:1), and for the multiplication of the loaves (Matt. 14:19), Jesus Christ lifted up His eyes to heaven. And David, in order to signify that he had prayed, said that he had "lifted his eyes up to heaven" (Ps. 121:1; 123:1). The Savior Himself even prayed to the Father with his knees on the ground (Luke 22:41), as the saints have often done (e.g., Dan. 6:10), and St. Paul indicated that he had prayed to God by saying no more than that he had bowed his knees "before the Father" (Eph. 3:14), so clearly does this ceremony belong to prayer. It was the solemn practice both of the Jews (e.g., 1 Kings 8:54) and of the first Christians (1 Tim. 2:8) to pray by raising the hands, which is, moreover, an entirely natural ceremony that almost every nation has employed, in order to recognize thereby that the heavens are the place of God's glory. As a witness, there is the one who said, "*Et duplices tendens ad sidera palmas,*" and, again, "*Corripio e stratis corpus, tendoque supinas / Ad coelum cum voce manus, et munera libo.*"[3]

The psalmist held it to be the same thing to pray as to lift up one's hands: "Let my prayer be counted as incense before you, and the lifting up of my hands as an evening sacrifice" (Ps. 141:2). Similarly, Moses said to Pharaoh: "As soon as I have gone out of the city, I will stretch out my hands to the Lord; the thunder will cease" (Exod. 9:29). The hand is also to be raised when one swears, for to swear an oath is nothing other than to invoke God as a witness (cf. Gen. 14:22), and, accordingly, when Ezra wanted to say that God had sworn, he said that God had lifted up His hand (cf. Neh. 9:15),[4] so commonplace was the ceremony of lifting a hand in the practice

---

[3] "And lifting his two hands to the stars" and "I dragged my body from bed and lifted the palms of my hands and my voice to heaven, and poured out an offering" (Virgil, *Aeneid*, I:93 and III:176–77).

[4] See 2 Esdras 9:15 in the Douay-Rheims edition, which closely follows the Latin of the Vulgate, the text of reference for St. Francis de Sales: "And thou saidst to them that they should go in, and possess the land, upon which thou hadst lifted up thy hand to give to them." The RSV says "to possess the land which you had sworn to give them."—Ed.

of oath-taking. When St. John described the oath of the angel, he said that he "lifted up his right hand to heaven" (Rev. 10:5). One can, therefore, most certainly pray by means of ceremonies. To be sure, the essence of prayer is in the soul, but the voice, our actions, and other external signs by which we express our interior state are the noble accompaniments and most useful qualities of prayer, for they are its effects and its works.

The soul will not be content to pray if the whole man does not. The soul, indeed, makes the eyes, the hands, and the knees pray along with it.

St. Antony, having entered the grotto of St. Paul, the first hermit, "saw the body of this saint without its soul, its knees bent, its head lifted, and its hands raised to heaven, and, at first thinking that he must still be alive and praying, betook himself to do the same; but not perceiving the sighs that the holy father was accustomed to make in prayer, he threw himself upon the body to kiss it with his tears, and knew that this dead body of the holy man, by its devout bearing and religious posture, was praying to the God by whom all things live and breathe." The soul that is prostrate before God pulls the body alongside it with ease, and it lifts the eyes to where it lifts the heart, and the hands to whence it awaits its help. Do we not thus understand the difference between the bearing and the countenance of the publican and the Pharisee (Luke 18:11, 13)?

By these examples, the words that the author of the treatise brings to bear against ceremonies are shown to be empty. "The service," he says, "that is due to the Divine Majesty should be paid to him according to his good pleasure and law. Now, the manifest will of God with respect to this subject is that we adore and serve him in spirit and in truth (John 4:24). And therefore, not only do we reject all of the Jewish ceremonies of old, but also all others that have been put forward in the Christian Church that are beyond and outside of the Word of God." He wants to give a reason why the Scriptures do not testify to the miracles made by the wood of the Cross, but instead of saying that it is because these miracles were accomplished long after the New Testament was written—which is the true and plain reason—he speaks in this way: "Certainly, it seems that there is no reason other than that God did not want to limit men to such earthly things, as St. Paul teaches us by saying that we should not know Jesus Christ according to the flesh (2 Cor. 5:16), and as he also says to the Colossians (Col. 3:1) that, serving God in the spirit, we should glory in Jesus Christ and not have any confidence in the flesh." Let us together see the poverty of these arguments.

The Legitimate Use of Ceremonies of Benediction

First, it is well known that these Reformed Christians observe a number of ceremonies and other customs that are beyond and outside of the written Word of God when solemnizing their marriages, performing their baptisms, and commemorating the Supper of the Lord. It is not because they are unscriptural, therefore, that they blame our ceremonies, but instead because they are not to their taste.

Second, if it is necessary to serve God according to His decrees, it is above all necessary to obey the Church and to maintain her customs; he who does otherwise, the Savior has pronounced to be "as a Gentile and a tax collector" (Matt. 18:17). And St. Paul, while teaching that men should pray with their heads uncovered and women with theirs covered—which is a purely ceremonial matter—anticipated those who would quarrel about it with these words: "we recognize no other practice, nor do the churches of God" (1 Cor. 11:16). He is not speaking the cant of the Evangelicals, but the true and simple Catholic language. He takes the custom of the Church of God to be a sufficient reason, for she understands her divine Spouse too well to establish anything disagreeable to Him.

Third, if in order to honor and to serve God in spirit and in truth it is necessary to reject those ceremonies that are not commanded in express terms in the Scriptures, then St. Paul should not have commanded men to pray uncovered and the women otherwise, inasmuch as he had no previous written commandment about it, nor should the Apostles have commanded new Christians to abstain "from what is strangled and from blood" (Acts 15:20). And why is it, you Reformers, that you pray with your hands together and kneeling? You will say that we have the example of Jesus Christ and the Apostles. But if their example has some power over you, why do you not wash one another's feet before the Supper of the Lord, since our Lord not only gave an example of it but invited us to do the same (John 13)? Why do you not anoint your sick with oil, as the Apostles did (Mark 6:13; James 5:14)? Why do you not leave behind all your possessions and belongings according to their example? Why do you not celebrate the Supper of the Lord in the evening, that is, at dinnertime, instead of in the morning, at the time for breakfast?

Fourth, who has ever heard such an argument as this: we must pray in spirit and in truth; therefore we must not pray with ceremonies? Are ceremonies indeed contrary to the spirit and the truth, so that one is banished through the establishment of the other? Who commanded Abraham, Aaron, Moses, David, St. Paul, St. Peter, and a thousand others to pray with their hands raised and their knees upon the earth? And were they thereby prevented from praying in spirit and in truth, or from being true worshippers? To interpret the Scriptures so ineptly is an ignorant effrontery. This is no reformed piety; this is formed impiety. So far is it from being the case that prayer in spirit and in truth need be without ceremonies, that the very contrary is true: the one who prays in spirit and in truth can only with difficulty omit the exterior actions and gestures that match the interior affections, so great a hold do the movements of the soul have upon the movements of the body. "I do not know how these movements of the body can be made," St. Augustine said, "if the movement of the spirit does not precede them, and, again, how when these movements are made externally, the invisible and interior motion could fail to grow, since the affection of the heart that precedes and produces these exterior movements grows because they are made and produced." A soul that has truly been moved is moved in every way: in the tongue, in the eyes, and in the hands. To pray in spirit and in truth is to pray with the heart and affections, without pretense or hypocrisy, and moreover to involve the whole man in it, soul and body, so that what God has joined should not be separated. I leave aside the true and straightforward interpretation of these words of our Lord, who set adoration in the spirit in opposition to the adoration of the Jews, which was almost entirely in figures, shadows, and exterior ceremonies, and the adoration in truth in opposition to the false, vain, heretical, and schismatic adoration of the Samaritans. There is no need for a lengthy discourse on that subject.

Fifth, if on account of St. Paul's teaching that we ought not to know Jesus Christ according to the flesh, we ought not to think about the Cross or other similar terrestrial things, why then do we recount the Passion and death of Jesus Christ, which belonged only to His flesh and to the time of His mortal life? What is it that you wish to say, my friend? That we ought not to know Jesus Christ according to the flesh? If you mean according to your flesh or that of other men, I confess it without reserve. But you would be thoughtless to reject the Cross for that reason, for the Cross is neither according to your flesh nor to mine: it is contrary to them both and their enemy. If you understand the text according to its evident meaning, which is to refer to the very flesh of Jesus Christ Himself, it is nevertheless unnecessary to say in an absolute way that we ought not know and recognize Jesus Christ according to the flesh. Was He not born of the Virgin according to the flesh? Did He not die, rise, and ascend into heaven according to the flesh? Is not His true flesh at the right hand of the Father? Is it not in truth His real flesh—or at the very least, and in accord with your vain fantasies, the *sign* of His flesh — that He gives us to eat? Is it, then, necessary to forget all of this, together with the *Verbum caro factum est* (John 1:14)? No. When St. Paul said that he did not know Jesus Christ according to the flesh, it was according to the same flesh that he spoke of when he said that "in the days of his flesh, Jesus offered up prayers and supplications" (Heb. 5:7) to the Father, in which the word *flesh* is taken to indicate mortality, infirmity, and the ability to suffer, as if he had said that Jesus Christ, during the days of His mortality, infirmity, and suffering offered prayers and supplications to the Father. In this way, in saying that he no longer knew Jesus Christ according to the flesh, he meant nothing other than that he no longer knew Jesus Christ as suffering and mortal — the natural qualities of the flesh — and, in a word, that he no longer knew him according to the flesh with its infirmities and natural condition.

Sixth, it is just as unreasonably that he adduces the third chapter of St. Paul's letter to the Colossians, for, either the words that he ascribes to the text are not there at all, or, if they are, they do not contradict us, inasmuch as we too confess that God must be served in the spirit and that we must glory in Jesus Christ and not put our confidence in our flesh. Yet all this in no way exempts the body or external actions from the contribution that we owe to the service of God. Now, perhaps he would allege what is said in the first verses of that chapter, and which have more in common with his argument: "If then you have been raised with Christ, seek the things that are above, where Christ is, seated at the right hand of God. Set your minds on things that are above, not on things that are on earth" (Col. 3:1–2). It hardly follows from these words that we must not set any value upon the Cross, the crèche, the tomb, and the other relics of our Lord that are here below on the earth. In truth, this passage would be useful against those whose intentions and desires are satisfied with things here below. "Seek the things that are above," we should indeed say to them: *sursum corda*. But our affections do not stop with the Cross or any other relic: we carry them to the kingdom of heaven, in quest of which we make use of all those things that can help us to lift our hearts toward Him whom we seek. We must climb to heaven, for that is where our regard is fixed, that is our final resting place, and the holy things here below serve as our ladders for the ascent.

Sailors, who navigate by the stars, do not for that sail to heaven, but upon the earth, nor do they look to the heavens for any reason other than to find the land. Christians, who sigh only for heaven, where their treasure is kept and which is the safe harbor of their hopes, quite often look here below, not because they seek the land, but in order to find the way to heaven. Seek Jesus Christ and what is above, you tell me. I do seek Him, truly, and so little do the Cross, the tomb, and the other holy things turn me away from Him—as you think—that instead they hasten and encourage my quest. Odors and tracks do not distract the good dog from its quarry; they embolden and enliven him. In the same way, by finding the Cross, the crèche, the tomb—these traces and scents of my Savior—I am all the more moved and drawn to this blessed quest: He pulls me along by the aroma of His anointing.

Here I am, then, finished with this importunate man on the subject of ceremonies in general. It is time now to achieve what I have set out to do.

Chapter 5

The Sign of the Cross in Blessings

Since to pray by means of a holy and legitimate ceremony is permissible, should we not pray by the Sign of
the Cross?

Let us begin to answer by speaking of the blessing of
created things according to the custom of the Church,
which blessings are nothing other than prayers and good
wishes by which we ask God to bestow some grace and
benefit upon the creature over which we stand in some
relation of superiority, for it is "beyond dispute that the
inferior is blessed by the superior" (Heb. 7:7). Let us now
demonstrate the use of the Sign of the Cross in such
blessings.

Under the Old Law, in which everything was done
as a type and a foreshadowing of what was to come, the
ordinary blessing made by the priests had—among other
parts—two external components. The first was that the
priest made use of certain determinate words:

The Sign of the Cross

The Lord bless you and keep you:
The Lord make his face to shine upon you,
    and be gracious to you:
The Lord lift up his countenance upon you,
    and give you his peace. (Num. 6:24–26)

The other was that the priest raised his hand, a point easily verified from the practice we see in the Scriptures: "Aaron lifted up his hands toward the people and blessed them" (Lev. 9:22). This custom takes its origin from the law of nature, as is apparent from the blessing that Jacob gave to his children (Gen. 48:14–15), which still endured in the time of our Lord, about whom St. Matthew said that the Jews brought children to Him "that he might lay his hands on them and pray" (Matt. 19:13), that is, that He might bless them. And this same fact St. Mark testifies to explicitly, saying that Jesus Christ "took them in his arms and blessed them, laying his hands upon them" (Mark 10:16).

These two things are still to be found today in ecclesiastical blessings, but with a clearer manifestation of the mysteries they contain. First, we invoke the name of the Father, and of the Son, and of the Holy Spirit, which is what was formerly accomplished under a veil. For what, I ask you, was the import of the three-fold repetition "The

The Sign of the Cross in Blessings

Lord bless you, the Lord make his face to shine upon you, the Lord lift up his countenance upon you" if not to point to the mystery of the most Blessed Trinity? The blessing of David was just the same: "God, our God, has blessed us. God has blessed us" (Ps. 67:7–8).

Second, in the place of the former custom of simply raising or imposing the hands, now we make the Sign of the Cross in order to attest that every blessing takes its merit and value from the Passion of Jesus Christ, which may also be called His exaltation. The Evangelical will be hard-pressed to reply. For if we raise our hand to bless, it is in imitation of the Savior, who, ascending to heaven, blessed the disciples by raising His hands (Luke 24:50). And if we make the Sign of the Cross, it is to show whence our blessings take their power and strength. Jacob already approached this form of blessing (cf. Gen. 48:14) when he crossed his hands while blessing the sons of Joseph, in order to prefer the younger to the elder, thus foreshadowing our Lord, who, with His arms on the Cross, blessed the world in such a way that the Gentiles effectively were favored over the Jews.

Yet, our Evangelical may ask, since the Savior did not use the Sign of the Cross when blessing His Apostles, why do you use it? To tell the truth, I do not know whether the Savior used it or not, for the Scriptures neither assure us of it nor deny it. But neither do I know whether the Crucified Himself, while blessing, had any need to use the Sign of the Cross: did He need to invoke Himself or attest that the blessing came from Him? What is more, the Sign of the Cross was sufficiently present in our Lord's own hands without His making any motion. What were those holes and punctures that He had in His hands, even after His Resurrection, if not the very marks and signs of the Cross? What need would He have had, therefore, to make any others? But Christians, raising their hands in order to bless, have every reason to make the Sign of the Cross, in order to show that they pretend to no blessing other than those which come by means of the exaltation of our Lord upon the Cross.

Now let us consider the sure proofs that this custom was widely followed in the Church of the Fathers. St. John Chrysostom, for one, said that "everything that contributes to our salvation is brought to fulfillment in the Cross." St. Dionysius, speaking of the consecration of priests, said that "while blessing, the bishop imprints the Sign of the Cross on each of them." St. Cyprian attested that "without this sign, there is nothing that is holy." St. Hilarion blessed with his hand those who needed to be delivered from an evil spirit, while Rufinus named a dozen hermits "by whose hands he had the honor of being blessed." St. Augustine visited a sick man at whose home he found the bishop, and he there "received the bishop's blessing," a blessing that was doubtless made with the Sign of the Cross.

The praetor of the East, as Theodoret recounted the episode, having newly entered his jurisdiction, wished to demolish a temple of Jupiter in accord with the power he had been given by Constantine, but he found the temple so well mortared together and bound with iron and lead that no human power could take it apart. A certain man, however, took up the task by undermining the principal columns of the building, putting wooden staging in place to hold them up and planning to set fire to them all at once so that the columns would fall. But the Devil, in a dark and frightful form, came to quench the fire's power. This was at once reported to Bishop Marcel, who ran into the church and called for water, which he had placed at the altar. Then, prostrate upon the earth, he prayed to our sweet Lord that He would not allow impiety to make such gains, and, making the Sign of the Cross upon the water, he commanded his deacon Equitius to run and sprinkle the fire with this holy water, which he did. All of a sudden, the Devil fled, for he could not withstand the power of this water. The fire was ignited by this water, which, although the very contrary of fire, acted as if it were oil, and soon all the wood was burned and the columns, now lacking their support, fell and brought the rest of the temple down with them. The roar of the destruction was heard throughout the city, and the people who had gathered around the spectacle saw the flight of the evil one and began to praise Almighty God.

A gentleman named Joseph, according to St. Epiphanius, wanted to build a church in the city of Tiberias. For this purpose he needed a great deal of cement and so had some seven furnaces built to extract it from limestone. But some enemies employed spells to prevent the fires from burning or even lighting. When Joseph realized it, he took a large jar full of water and before the large crowd of Jews there watching, he cried aloud and made the Sign of the Cross with his own hand and invoked the name of Jesus, saying: "In the name of Jesus of Nazareth, whom my fathers crucified, may this water be given the power to release every charm and enchantment made by these people." Then he took the water in his hand and sprinkled every furnace, and immediately the spells were destroyed and the flames leapt forth for everyone to see, to which the people who were present gave a great cry: "There is only one God, the one who gives help to the Christians."

The mother of St. Gregory Nazianzen was ill and could not eat, and there was a great risk that she would die for want of nourishment. Here is how St. Gregory himself recounted how she was helped and fed. "It seemed to her," he wrote, "that I had come to her in the night with a basket and that I handed her bread that was very white, blessed, and signed according to my ordinary custom, and that she was thus healed and regained her strength. And this vision of the night was followed with truth, for henceforward she returned to herself and conceived of a better hope, as was generally recognized." The ordinary custom of which this great and ancient theologian speaks was that of making the Sign of the Cross over the meal.

Next to the statue of him that was placed in the Forum, Julian the Apostate had painted an image of Jupiter descending from the heavens to bring him his crown and his robes of imperial purple, with Mars and Mercury on either side of him, looking at him as if to testify that he was a man both courageous and eloquent, so that, under the pretext of enforcing the law to honor himself, Julian would force his subjects implicitly to honor the painted idols as well. Here was his thinking: if he could persuade the Christians to honor the idols, his cause would already be won, but if they gave him trouble about it, he could take the occasion to avenge himself upon them as offenders against the customs of Rome, for their refusal would offend both the emperor and the republic.

Now, the few who saw through this trickery and did not want to adore the image of the emperor placed between the idols were in the end martyred. The common people, however, acting in good faith and thinking only to honor the emperor, made their reverence before these idols.

But the emperor, wishing to push his plan still further, had his soldiers who were due to be paid brought to him, and he commanded them to cast incense upon the fire that was before the idols as they received their pay, as if it were an ordinary Roman military ceremony. Some of them, discovering the trick, refused to commit the impiety. Some others who were not so quick-witted did what they were commanded to do without further thought. Still others, either by avarice or by fear, allowed themselves to commit the sinful act.

Now, some of those who had done the deed through ignorance and thoughtlessness found themselves at table together that night, raising the glass to one another, as was their custom, and invoking Jesus Christ upon their drink and making the Sign of the Cross. At this point, one of them asked the others how they dared to invoke Jesus Christ and make His sign, seeing as how they had renounced Him just a short while before. These men, now understanding the trick that had been played upon

The Sign of the Cross in Blessings

them, went out into the streets to cry out sorrowfully that they had been betrayed, that they had committed paganism only with their hands, and that their hearts had been entirely free from the deed. Coming to the emperor, they threw at his feet the bags of silver he had given them, asking to be punished with the death sentence for the crime that they had committed, although unwittingly. Upon hearing this, the emperor, although extremely out of temper, did not want to have them killed, for fear that he would thereby make martyrs of them, but merely wanted them to be fired from their jobs. Sozomen, who recounted this episode, did not say that they made the Sign of the Cross (which I mention so that my adversary, who often makes mistakes of fact, will not think that I have made one); it was St. Gregory Nazianzen who added that detail.

Nor should we think it strange if these good soldiers made the Sign of the Cross before drinking, for of old it was the custom to bless not only the table and the meal, but also each course separately and also the drink. As witness the delightful history written by St. Gregory of Tours about a heretical priest who wanted to prevent a good Roman Catholic priest who was at table with him not only from blessing but also from eating, and having effectively done so with the first three dishes brought to the table, with the fourth and last, having made the sign (for the character of his heresy did not extend, as that of the Reformers did, to the rejection of the Sign of the Cross), he placed the first morsel in his mouth. It was so hot that he died of it, while emitting a great noise, which gave occasion to our author to say, "His memory perished with a noise" (cf. Ps. 9:7 [Douay-Rheims]). The host who was entertaining the two men became a Catholic on the spot.

Similarly, St. John Chrysostom attested that the Sign of the Cross was made "*in symposiis et thalamis,*" that is to say, at feasts and the marriage bed. Tertullian added, "at baths, at table, and upon candles." Ephraim said, "whether one eats or drinks," and Cyril, "eating bread and drinking the cup." Moreover, evil often befalls those who have disdained to make the holy sign before eating and drinking: witness the nun who ate a lettuce and the monk who drank without making the Sign of the Cross, both of whom were immediately seized by evil spirits. My adversary makes two reproaches to these accounts. "Who does not see," he asks, "that the first is a fable?" And as to the other, "St. Paul said that our meat is sanctified for us by the Word of God and by prayer and says nothing of the Sign of the Cross." He is wrong, for these accounts have nothing suspect about them, and they come from a trustworthy source, St. Gregory the Great, who is worth more than all the Reformers both in doctrine and in authority. Will it be permitted to contradict the Fathers in this way? What is more, the dictum of St. Paul that our meats are made holy by our prayers (1 Tim. 4:3–5) confirms what we have said. The Sign of the Cross is a brief, easy, powerful, and ordinary prayer for the blessing of meat; to say that the Devil seized a monk and a nun for failure to pronounce the Sign of the Cross is to say that it was for failure to pray the easiest, most familiar prayer, and one for which the strongest reason could be alleged. As we shall see, the Sign of the Cross has a particular power against the devils, beyond the power that is common to all prayer.

Chapter 6

The Sign of the Cross in Consecrations and Sacramental Blessings

As the Fathers have told us, it was the Savior's side, pierced by the lance while He was on the Cross, that was the living fountain whence flowed all of the graces given to the faithful through the holy sacraments. Where ought the Sign of the Cross, therefore, be more frequently used than to attest that the Passion is the spring of living water that the sacraments bring to us? Consecrations are the most excellent invocations made by the Church. The holy sign, being so fitting a means of prayer, cannot be better employed than in consecrating; thus the Sign of the Cross was the ordinary form for consecrations in the Church of the Fathers. Let us listen to the witnesses.

St. John Chrysostom: "The Cross shines forth from the holy Table at the ordination of priests as well as with the Body of Jesus Christ in the Mystical Supper." And elsewhere, speaking of the Cross, he said: "Everything that conduces to our salvation is summed up by it, for being regenerated, the Cross is there when we are nourished with the holiest of food, when we are consecrated in Holy Orders: in everything and everywhere this standard of victory comes to our aid."

St. Augustine: "If this sign were not applied to the forehead of believers, or to the water with which they are regenerated, or to the chrism oil with which they are anointed, or to the sacrifice by which they are nourished, none of these would be as perfect as they should be."

St. Cyprian: "We glory in the Cross of the Lord, the power of which perfects all of the sacraments, without the sign of which nothing is holy, nor is any consecration effectual." And elsewhere he said: "Whosoever be the administrator of the sacraments, whosoever be the hands to bathe and anoint those who are baptized, whosoever be the chest from which the sacred words come forth: the authority and the effect of all the sacraments is in the figure of the Cross."

St. Dionysius testified that the chrism was poured out in the baptistery in the form of the Cross, as we still do today. Treating holy anointing, he said that "the bishop begins the anointing with the Sign of the Holy Cross, leaving the man to the priests to be anointed on his body by them." And of Holy Orders: "On each of the men the

Sign of the Cross is impressed by the bishop who blesses them."

St. Clement explained how the earliest prelates of Christianity signed themselves with the Cross as they approached the altar: "Then the bishop, praying in a place apart together with his priests, puts on a splendid, shining robe and, remaining standing toward the altar, signs himself on his forehead with the sign of victory, the Cross, as he says, 'The grace of almighty God, and the love of our Lord Jesus Christ, and the communion of the Holy Spirit be with you all.'"

St. Augustine mentioned the custom of signing children at Baptism when he said that from the womb of his mother he was already marked with the Sign of the Cross and seasoned with its salt, by which he meant that the mother destined the child for Baptism, at which he was marked with the Cross and given salt.

My opponent almost sees this, but he can never bring himself to speak the truth plainly. In the liturgies of St. James and of St. John Chrysostom, the priest is often commanded to make the Sign of the Cross. In St. Basil's, not only does the priest make the Sign of the Cross over the offerings, but he also makes it three times over the people in the same form as our episcopal blessings.

And that should suffice.

Chapter 7

Why the Sign of the Cross
Is Made on the Forehead

In the age of the Fathers, the Sign of the Cross was made on all the parts of the body. "Let us paint this life-giving standard on our doors," said St. Ephraim, "on our foreheads, on our mouth, on our chest, and on all our limbs." Nevertheless we ordinarily sign ourselves on our forehead. This I have had occasion to mention, but now I will give the reasons for the custom.

Here is the first, in the very words of St. Augustine: "In order to banish the shame of the Cross, I will not keep it in a secret place, but I will wear it on my forehead. We receive the sacraments in different ways: some we take in the mouth, as you know, and some in the body as a whole. Now, because our shame is worn on our forehead, the one who said, 'He who is ashamed of me before men, I will be ashamed of before my father in heaven' [Matt. 10:33; Luke 9:26], has placed upon the place of shame and modesty the same ignominious sign that the pagans disdain. When you hear a man responding to some impudence by saying that he is affronted, what does it mean? That he has no forehead, that is, that he has been shamed. Now that is why I do not have a naked forehead, but one covered by the Cross of my Savior."

Here is the second reason: "The posts of the houses of Israel were anointed and soaked in blood to ward off the angel [cf. Exod.12:22–23]. The Christian peoples are marked with the sign of the Savior's Passion as a preservative unto salvation." These are once again the words of St. Augustine, by which he showed that just as the children of Israel marked the posts and lintels of their homes with the blood of the Paschal lamb in order to be safe from extermination, so also Christians are marked on their foreheads—the lintel of the whole man—with the sign of the blood and of the Passion of the Lamb who takes away the sins of the world (John 1:29), that they might be safe from all of the enemies of their salvation. Lactantius made the same point in a well-turned phrase. St. Ephraim mentioned it in his book *On True Penitence*, and St. Cyprian said it explicitly in his second book to Quirinus.

My opponent takes note of this argument as made by St. Augustine and Lactantius and offers this censure of it: "Be that as it may, it was a practice introduced in imitation of the Jewish example and not according to a commandment. Now, we ought never to found anything upon the example of men alone or upon general rules inferred from God's commandments. The Israelites had a commandment from God to do what they did on their lintels, but Christians were not commanded to sign themselves on their foreheads. And so a most pernicious error has spread: born first from their foolish simplicity, then growing in their ignorance, and today defended by stubbornness, the error of attributing to the wood of the Cross what is proper to the Crucified alone."

This is what my opponent has to say. I have several things to say in reply.

First, in his desire to censure the Fathers for having approved an unwritten ceremony, my adversary brings forward no authority in support of himself. Having no written commandment to make the Sign of the Cross, he will not make it. Having no written prohibition of it, I will not cease to make it.

Second, it is a proof of ignorance or folly to say one ought never to establish anything upon the example of men or upon general rules inferred from God's commandments. Where, for instance, is it commanded that we pray kneeling? Calvin was unable to find a text other than the one in which the Apostle says, "All things should be done decently and in order" (1 Cor. 14:40).[5] Let us, I pray you, consider this reasoning: All things should be done decently and in order; therefore, it is necessary to kneel while praying. What then? Would it not be decent and orderly to be seated, standing, or prostrate upon the ground? Why would it not be decent to sign oneself on the forehead? By what commandment did Isaac and Jacob bless their children (Gen. 27:27; 49:28)? By what commandment did St. John [the Baptist] wear such lowly garments, live in the desert instead of in his father's house, drink neither wine nor strong drink, and eat only locusts and wild honey (Matt. 3:4)? As to his belt, he imitated Elijah, but without a commandment to do so. And yet these are things that the Evangelists deemed noteworthy and saw fit to document. When Elisha struck the waters with his master's coat (2 Kings 2:14), by what commandment did he do so? Was it not done to imitate his master, who had done the same thing not long before (2 Kings 2:8)? To lift up and to lay on the hands in order to bless: where was this commanded? And yet the practice is witnessed to by the whole of the Scriptures.

[5] See John Calvin, *Institutes of the Christian Religion*, IV.10.§30, trans. Ford Lewis Battles (Philadelphia: Westminster Press, 1960), 1207–1208.

Why the Sign Is Made on the Forehead

Third, it is a falsehood to say that Christians have not been commanded to sign themselves on the forehead. Here are my arguments to prove that they have.

Inasmuch as the Sign of the Cross is a profession of faith and an invocation of the Crucifixion, we are, in effect, commanded to sign ourselves on the forehead wherever we are commanded to profess the faith and to invoke Jesus Christ. Yet, my opponent will say, one can pray to God in other ways. I admit it, but I say that one can also pray in this way just as well as by lifting one's hands and eyes.

And insofar as the general commandments to pray to God and to confess the Faith do not prohibit the Sign of the Cross, why do they wish to prohibit us from using it? Calvin admitted that no text can be brought forward to prove that the Apostles ever baptized an infant but nevertheless boldly said: "This does not prove that they were not baptized, seeing as how children are never excluded when there is mention of a family being baptized."[6] Similarly, we cannot show that the prayer made by the Sign of the Cross was expressly commanded, but this does not indicate that it was not commanded; it was never excluded when we were commanded to pray.

[6] Calvin, *Institutes*, IV.16.§8.

If the figure is commanded, the thing prefigured is also recommended, inasmuch as the figure is practiced only to recommend the thing prefigured and to assure us of its eventual coming. Now, if we ought more readily to follow St. Cyprian, St. Augustine, St. Ephraim, and the other Fathers than the author of this treatise, we can affirm with them that the sprinkling of the posts and lintels was the prefigurement of the sign made on the forehead of Christians. If, therefore, the figure was commanded to the Jews, then Christians have a sufficient foundation to hold that the thing thus prefigured is commanded to them.

Circumcision, a figure of Baptism, was commanded for little children under the Old Law (Lev. 12:3). Calvin sees no difficulty in founding upon this commandment made in prefigurement a proof of the practice of infant Baptism against the Anabaptists.[7] Why, then, is it not allowable for St. Augustine and the other Fathers to draw forth as a consequence of the mark of the blood of the lamb upon the entrance of houses the duty that we have to mark our foreheads, as being the lintel of our earthly habitation, with the sign of the holy Passion? This surely is a sufficient command.

[7] Calvin, *Institutes*, IV.16.§4-5.

Why the Sign Is Made on the Forehead

Although it is not said explicitly in Scripture, the Apostles did leave it in that other part of Christian doctrine, tradition. "Whatever the business at hand, we touch our forehead with the Sign of the Cross. If you ask for the written commandment of this observance, you will not find one, and you will have tradition brought forward as authority, confirming our custom and observing our faith." These are the words of Tertullian. And a few years later St. Basil said: "We have several articles that are preached in the Church about the written doctrine, and we also receive several others from the tradition that the Apostles left in mystery," that is, as a secret, "which two have equal force for piety, and which no one will contradict who knows even a little about the rights of the Church. For if we attempt to reject unwritten customs as being unimportant, we will imprudently condemn things in the Gospel that are necessary to salvation. We would thus render contemptible the preaching of the Faith. One such custom is that by which we mark with the Sign of the Cross those who have put their faith in Jesus Christ: whoever taught this in writing?" Have you, my opponent, ever heard this great and ancient teacher tell how he holds the observance of signing oneself on the forehead as a commandment, even though it has never been explicitly written down? How will you oppose him, seeing as how he is a man according to your taste? Certainly he is a man, and a most zealous one and well-versed in the new law of the Gospel as it was observed by the Church during the time of its greatest purity. The Church was then, as St. Gregory of Nyssa called it, "a magnificent trumpet and voice, and the eye of the world." This is just one bishop, but he is an intelligent one and in accord with the doctrine and ecclesiastical discipline of his colleagues.

Finally, I would like to hear from my adversary at what point he thinks the error of attributing to the wood what is proper to the Crucified emerged. If he means the honor paid to the Cross, as it is done in the Catholic Church, he will not be able to show when it was born, for it has always been; and it is inept to say that it was born from foolish simplicity. Although St. Ambrose, St. Paulinus, St. Augustine, and a thousand other such Fathers who have taught this honor, were in truth simple as doves, they were also, and equally, as wise as serpents, so much so that their holy simplicity could never give birth to any error. This is the insult that these innovators give to the Fathers, and attributing the error to their simplicity does not make it less of an insult. For a simplicity that is erring and is a mother of errors is called folly when it is found in those who have charge of the people. And nevertheless my opponent spreads calumny, saying that they attributed to the wood of the Cross what is proper to the Crucified. We have never thought to do that, nor have we ever done so. Moreover, it is a clever move that this fellow makes, saying that the error of honoring the Cross was "born of foolish simplicity, grew by ignorance, and is defended to-day by stubbornness." For thus he attributes knowledge with stubbornness to our era, simple ignorance to our predecessors, and, to the earliest Christians, an ignorant simplicity, insofar as no other simplicity could be a cause of error. While, on the contrary, these Fathers, far-seeing as they were, would have been the more blameworthy if they had given rise to this error. Then it would be us who would err by simplicity and ignorance in following them. But I am toying too much with this long-winded fellow.

The third reason we sign ourselves on our forehead was touched on by St. Jerome: "The priest of the Old Law carried a plate of the finest gold attached to his ti-ara, hanging on the forehead, on which was engraved 'Holy unto the Lord,' and he had always to keep this on his forehead so that God would be kindly to him (Exod. 28:36–38). What was formerly shown in the plate of gold is shown by us with the Sign of the Cross; the blood of the Gospel is more precious than the gold of the Law." In order to show that Christians, being a royal priesthood (1

Pet. 2:9), are holy to the Lord by the blood of the Savior, in place of the plate of gold they carry the Sign of the Cross on their forehead.

And there are still other reasons noted by Origen and St. John Chrysostom. The Sign of the Cross is our standard, and so it should be mounted on the most visible part of our city. It is our trophy, and so it should be raised up to the highest part of our temple, as upon an honorable column. It is our crown, and so it should be upon our heads. It is our escutcheon, and so it should be upon our door and upon the front of our house. It is an honorable mark, and so we should make it with the right hand, as being the more noble, and we should place it upon the most illustrious part of our bodies. And there are a thousand other such reasons from the Fathers.

Chapter 8

The Testimony of the Prophet Ezekiel

God "called to the man clothed in linen, who had the writing case at his side," says the prophet Ezekiel. "And the Lord said to him, 'Go through the city, through Jerusalem, and mark *tau* upon the foreheads of the men who sigh and groan over all the abominations that are committed in it.'" And immediately afterward he commanded the six men who each carried a deadly weapon in his hand to massacre all those they were to find in the city. "But," he said, "touch no one upon whom is the mark" (Ezek. 9:3–6). This *tau*, the mark of safety, signified nothing other than the Cross. Now, it was marked on the forehead, and that is why we make the Cross on our foreheads. It is a pretty proof of the honor and power of the Cross, and such a weighty one that the author of the treatise attempts to obscure its meaning. Let us see what he has to say and then examine the matter ourselves.

The Sign of the Cross

Having recited the text of Ezekiel in this way, "mark the mark on the foreheads of the men," he continues thus: "It is in this sense and with these words that the Greek translator has it, as also St. Jerome notes the Septuagint interprets it, and Aquila and Symmachus have said the same, that is to say, 'Put the sign or the mark on their foreheads.' For *tau* in Hebrew signifies a mark or a sign, and is taken from the word *thavah*, to signify or to design." This is no great news. A thousand of our own scholars have already noted it. But what consequence can be drawn from it against us?

Let us grant that this translation is the best. Will we not still have the same advantage that the Sign of the Cross—the most excellent of pure and simple signs and the great sign of the Son of Man—can be understood more fittingly than any other under the word *mark* or *sign* taken absolutely? For in this way, even though it may be possible to have several signs of the Son of Man, when one speaks absolutely about the Sign of the Son of Man, the Fathers understood this to mean the Sign of the Cross.

St. Jerome, taking the sign of Ezekiel not for the letter *tau* simply but merely as a sign and a mark in general, did not for that fail to apply it to the Cross. "According to the word of Ezekiel," he said, "the sign was attached to the foreheads of the men who sigh and groan; now, carrying the Cross, we say, 'The light of thy countenance, O Lord, is signed upon us'" (Ps. 4:7 [Douay-Rheims]). Thus when it says in the book of Revelation (Rev. 7:3), "Do not harm the earth or the sea or the trees, till we have sealed the servants of our God upon their foreheads," the mark in question is none other than the Cross, as Rupert, Anselm, and others have advanced, and with good reason. For what mark could one carry on the forehead that would be honorable before God the Father other than that of His Son? And to what kind of mark can we say these texts point other than the one with which all the greatest servants of God have been marked and of which they have been so justly proud?

After my adversary thus gave his opinion about the version of this text, he continued in this way: "It is true that the Vulgate has retained the word *tau*, taking it materially (as the philosophers would put it), about which several have speculated at their pleasure. For some, as St. Jerome himself tells us, have said that the letter *tau*, which is the last letter of the Hebrew alphabet, signified those who had perfect understanding; others have said that the same letter indicates the Law, which in Hebrew is called Torah, a word whose first letter is *tau*. Finally, the same St. Jerome, setting aside the letter used by the prophet, looked into the Samaritan alphabet, and said that *tau*, to the Samaritans, resembles a cross, but he does not paint an image of this Samaritan *tau*. And, sensing that his own friends will accuse him of obscure investigations, he immediately afterward employs another expression, when he says that the letter *tau*, because the last in the alphabet, represented those upright men who were the remnant, as it were, of the evil multitudes of the living."

That is my adversary's second argument, and to it I have several things to say.

First, the ancient Vulgate edition merits this honor: that we not be quick to set it aside for any other, and, inasmuch as it retains the word *tau* for the mark that was to be marked upon those who groaned, we ought not to reject *tau* lightly.

Second, it is wrong to say that several have speculated about this subject "at their pleasure," referring to the considerations of the Fathers about this prophecy. For their weighty minds did not mold the Scriptures to their pleasure, but their pleasure to the Scriptures.

Third, even though St. Jerome gave several senses of the passage, they were not contradictory, but can all be founded together upon the one that St. Jerome thought the most presentable and the most straightforward: for the fullness of knowledge, signified by the last of—and so the fullness of—letters, which is *tau*, lies in knowing and practicing the Law, which is also signified by *tau*, inasmuch as the word *Torah*, which means the Law, begins with *tau*. Now, the Law is not kept except by the remnant, that is, by the few who are good, and their goodness comes from the power of the Cross and death of the Savior, the sign of which is on their foreheads, expressed by the Hebrew letter *tau*. This is to philosophize for God's honor and not for private pleasure.

Fourth, we must be careful of our treatise writer, who by a ruse wants to make us believe that St. Jerome thought his third interpretation may have pushed his investigations too far, but that he then went on to offer a fourth. Truly, this is falsehood, for the last interpretation is much more strained than the third. What does the last letter of the alphabet have to do with the just remnant of the human race? St. Jerome himself said that the Hebrew letter *tau* is indeed similar to the Cross. He elsewhere repeated his third interpretation, which suffices to prove that he thought it reasonable. He also openly protested that it was his own opinion, for, having alleged the first two, he set out the third one in these terms: "But so that we may come to our own business: according to the ancient alphabet of the Hebrews, which the Samaritans still use today, the last letter — *tau* — resembles the Cross, which is painted on the forehead of Christians and signed by the inscription frequently made with the hand."

My adversary then once again opposes our argument about the prophecy of Ezekiel, citing the supposed disproportion between the Cross and the ancient Hebrew letter *tau*. "Although it be granted," he says, "that the letter *tau* was painted in the Hebrew style, or that of the Samaritans, it is easy to see that there is little likeness between it and a whole cross: the Hebrew letter is made this way, ת, while the Samaritan letter is made thus, T, for what is missing is the upper part, where the writing or title of the Cross was attached, as has been noted by Lipsius in his book on the Cross." Is there not great subtlety here?

There is little likeness, he says, between the *tau*, T, and a whole cross, †. But what greater likeness could there be other than the *tau* being itself a cross? To be sure, we do not say that the *tau* is a cross, but that it resembles one. Now, *similia non sunt eadem*.[8] It is not a cross, but the difference is slight.

He is also wrong to allege that the Hebrew letter is made like this ת, for that is the letter as it is made to-day — about which we have nothing to say — while the

---

[8] Similar things are not the same.

one that was made in the time of Ezekiel, as St. Jerome says, resembles a cross.

And as to the Samaritan letter, I do not know whether it is the same today as it was in the time of St. Jerome. This I can well believe: if it no longer has the form of a cross, that the Jews and the rabbis could have changed it in hatred of the Cross, which they detest so much that they are unwilling to name it, as I have said elsewhere.

"But," says my opponent, "after the words we must come to the meaning. And first, it is apparent from what is told in the eighth and ninth chapters of Ezekiel that everything said there was represented as a vision in his mind, which means that the deeds were not really done." I willingly concede this point and say that this vision, being spiritual, has that much more to do with the spirit of the gospel than with the body of the Old Law, and that the deed that was not really done in the old, material Jerusalem should be really verified in the new, Christian Jerusalem.

"In the second place," says the author of the treatise, "it is clear that this prophecy was properly and particularly addressed to the city of Jerusalem and that it was seen to be executed when the Babylonians took and razed the city of Jerusalem and carried off the survivors into captivity. It is, therefore, unreasonable that what was said for a certain time and place and for certain persons be turned aside and assigned elsewhere, which was never the intention of the Spirit of God that spoke through the mouth of Ezekiel."

Here I would indeed have much to say, but the following will suffice for my purposes.

Although these words of Ezekiel were immediately directed against Jerusalem, it is nevertheless a mark of ignorance to conclude that they should not be applied to the spiritual Jerusalem. How many prophecies are there that point to the truth of the Gospel but which with respect to their initial sense only touch upon what was done in the shadows and under the figure of the Old Law? There is Psalm 72: "Give the king your justice, O God," the whole of which looks to our Savior and his royalty, even though it was immediately directed toward Solomon, who served as a shadow and image to represent Jesus Christ, the Prince of eternal peace. Again, there is what is said in the Book of Samuel: "I will be his father, and he shall be my son" (2 Sam. 7:14). Is it not evident that the passage primarily and literally refers to King Solomon, the son of Bathsheba? Nevertheless, it also can be referred to the Savior of the world, unless in order to save your inept interpretation, you will also reject the letter to the Hebrews, where this text is formally applied to Jesus

Christ (Heb. 1:5); and the Gospel of John, where the words "Not a bone of him shall be broken" are applied to Jesus Christ (John 19:36) even though their immediate referent was the Paschal lamb (Exod. 12:46). Why, then, did Ezekiel direct his prophecy toward Jerusalem if it was not to be understood with respect to the mystery of the Church?

If only from reverence for the Fathers who referred Ezekiel's *tau* to the Cross, my adversary should have spent years inquiring into their reasons instead of saying insolently that the thing was unreasonable, that the text had been misinterpreted, and that it was never the intention of the Holy Spirit that it be understood in that way. Although we be unable to see the reason our Fathers were moved to say something, we ought not for that to judge them unreasonable. It would be better to say this instead: what I understand is beautiful, as also is that which they say that I do not understand. Now, just how many of the Fathers referred Ezekiel's *tau* to the Cross?

Origen: "The massacre of the holy people began, and the only ones who were saved were those who had been marked by the letter *tau*, that is to say, with the image of the Cross."

Tertullian: "The Greek letter *tau*, and our own *T*, resemble the Cross, which, as they foretold," he said, speaking of Ezekiel, "should be on our foreheads, which are turned toward the true and Catholic Jerusalem."

St. Cyprian: "That the Sign of the Cross would be the salvation of all who would be marked by it on their forehead, God told Ezekiel, saying: you will go through Jerusalem and you will mark this sign upon those who groan."

St. John Chrysostom: "The mystery of the Cross is shown in the number three hundred, for the letter T is the mark of the three hundred, of whom it is said in Ezekiel: and you will write the *tau* upon the foreheads of those who groan, and whomever shall have it written upon him will not be killed, for whomever has the standard of the Cross on his forehead cannot be injured by the Devil."

St. Jerome said the same thing explicitly, as I have noted earlier.

St. Augustine, in his *Questions on the Book of Judges*, where he treats of the three hundred, also related the letter T to the mystery of the Cross. I could bring forward several others, but here we have the very flower of the Fathers, including Origen, Chrysostom, and Jerome, who knew so well the languages in which the words of Scripture were written. How is it, then, that our adversary has dared to treat with contempt our argument about Ezekiel, which was itself laid out so well by these learned and venerable masters?

Let us move on to my adversary's next claim. "It will never be proven," he says, "that the Jews were marked on the forehead with any mark whatsoever, and still less with the Cross, which was something that all the people regarded as hateful and ignoble."

Here I call a halt and summon my adversary to tell me whether the words of Ezekiel mean that those who groaned would be marked on their foreheads? It cannot be denied. Either, then, they were marked, and then he speaks falsely by saying that they never were, or they were not marked, and then I ask when is it that the prophecy will be shown to be true in its very words? If it was not in the temporal Jerusalem, then it will be in the spiritual Jerusalem, which is the Church. Truly, these ancient visions, foreshadowings, and prophecies are never so perfectly carried out upon the first subject to which they are addressed, as they are in the last and final subject to which they are referred by mystical understanding, as St. Augustine most excellently explains in the passage I have already cited. Thus the lines of Psalm 72, the book of Samuel, and Exodus that I have pointed out are more perfectly fulfilled in Jesus Christ, who was their last subject, than in Solomon or the Paschal lamb who were their first. Similarly when the Apostles apply prophecies and foreshadowings to our Savior or to the Church, they ordinarily make use of this phrase: "so that what was written might be fulfilled" (Matt. 27:35 [Douay-Rheims]). If the Jews were not marked with *tau*, as my adversary would have it, I conclude that in order to maintain the truth of this vision, it was necessary that the Christians, that is, the spiritual Israelites, be thus marked, that is to say, with the Cross, which was signified by the *tau*.

Nevertheless, my opponent continues in this way: "Now then, the true meaning of the passage of Ezekiel is that God declared that when this great judgment would be carried out upon the city of Jerusalem, only those would be spared who would be marked by the Spirit of God; and this manner of speaking is taken from the eleventh chapter of Exodus, where it is commanded to the Israelites to place the blood of the lamb upon the lintels of their homes, so that the angel could see the mark of this blood and pass over without harming the Israelites. And also, in the seventh chapter of the book of Revelation, mention is made of those who are marked, who are elsewhere called those chosen by God, or those whom the Savior claims as his own, and whose names are written in the book of life. For 'it is God,' as St. Paul says, who 'has put his seal upon us and given us his Spirit in our hearts as a guarantee'" (2 Cor. 1:21–22).

To this, I reply: First, if we are to understand the prophecy in light of the mark of the blood of the lamb that was made upon the doorposts of the Israelites, then it ought to be referred to a real and external mark, for the lintels and posts were truly marked and signed.

Second, if the mark about the doorposts was a figure and foreshadowing of the Sign of the Cross, as I have demonstrated above, then the sign of Ezekiel, coming from that source, also should be referred to the Sign of the Cross as its accomplishment.

Third, those spoken of in the book of Revelation as having been marked give us still more assurance; they are those who for having made profession of their faith and for having invoked the Savior were marked with the Sign of the Cross, as the Fathers have interpreted the passage. For the elect are none other than those who will have confessed with their mouths, in their heart, by signs and by works, and to the extent to which they are able — together with the Apostle — that they have no glory other than the Cross of Jesus Christ (cf. Gal. 6:14). Truly, the very life's blood of our happiness is to be anointed and marked in our hearts by our Master, but the exterior sign is also required, inasmuch as it cannot be disdained without rejecting the interior one, and as our two parts both belong to Jesus Christ—the interior and the exterior—it is most reasonable that they should both carry his mark and sign.

Chapter 9

A Reproof to the Antichrist

After the author of the treatise has labored to establish that the mark of Ezekiel was invisible by referring to the mark of the elect spoken of in the book of Revelation, he then adduces the mark of the beast to the same end. Here are his words: "To the contrary is what is said in the sixteenth chapter of the book of Revelation, that the angel will pour out his bowl in order that 'foul and evil sores' should come upon those 'who bore the mark of the beast,' that is to say, the servants of the Antichrist" (Rev. 16:2). But truly, all this only further strengthens what the Fathers have said about Ezekiel, and here we shall find yet another reason Christians should willingly receive and make the Sign of the Cross upon their foreheads.

The Antichrist, that man of sin, that savage beast, wanting to tear down bit by bit the discipline of the Christian religion by establishing observances contrary to those of the faithful, will have his servants marked with a sign and thus impressed with a certain character. The book of Revelation says as much (Rev. 13:16), but what we need to know is whether this sign is visible and perceptible. The innovators say that it is not and that to be signed with the mark of the beast means nothing more than to accept and approve his abominations. They say as much, but they do not prove it.

Now, I say to the contrary that this mark will be apparent and visible, and here is my reasoning, which I think incontrovertible.

The words of the book of Revelation clearly signify a real and exterior mark, and there is no difficulty understanding them to mean as much: why, then, should I twist them into a unnatural meaning when their natural one is easily understood?

The Antichrist will be extremely proud, for which reason it would make sense that he would require his followers to wear a mark, just as the wealthy have their servants arrayed in livery.

The Devil, a spiritual being, is not content to receive the homage of sorcerers, but also impresses upon them a bodily mark, as a thousand witnesses and trial documents attest. Who can doubt that the man of sin, so exact a disciple of the Devil, will do the same and that he will not desire, as others before him have done, to have his servants bear his mark?

The martyr St. Hippolytus, together with Primasius, Bede, and Rupert, understood as much; here are his words, speaking of the Antichrist: "All those suffering from famine will hurry before him to adore him, and to them he will give a sign on their right hand and on their forehead, so that no one will be able to paint with his hand the precious Cross upon his forehead." He added: "Thus this seducer will give them something to sustain their lives, in return for his infamous seal and sign." And again: "He will set his seal upon those who obey him." Who can fail to see that obedience goes together with the sign? And who would not rather follow these dispassionate Fathers instead of these innovators who are entirely consumed by the desire to establish their fantasies upon some scriptural pretext?

But here is a still more insistent reason. St. John, speaking of the Antichrist, said explicitly in the thirteenth chapter of the book of Revelation, that "it causes all, both small and great, both rich and poor, both free and slave, to be marked on the right hand or the forehead, so that no one can buy or sell unless he has the mark, that is, the name of the beast or the number of its name" (Rev. 13:16–17). Does not the alternative "on the right hand or the forehead" show that it will be a perceptible mark, something beyond merely being a follower of the Antichrist? And unless it were visible, how could it signify the difference between those allowed to buy and sell and those who were not? How would one know who had the number or the name or the mark if it were in the heart?

Now, what is said in the sixteenth chapter of the book of Revelation refers back to what was said in the thirteenth. If in one of these places the mark of the Antichrist is described as visible, then it will also be visible and external in the other. The matter is entirely clear. It is, therefore, a misunderstanding to say that this mark of the Antichrist will not be real and perceptible. If the Antichrist, wanting to oppose Christ, shall mark his people on their forehead and thus oblige them never to sign themselves with the Cross, as Hippolytus said, with how much more affection ought we to hold on to the use of this holy sign in order to profess that we are Christians and that we will never obey the Antichrist?

The Evangelical ministers have taught their people that ecclesiastical crowns are the mark of the beast, but seeing that they were not able to bring forward a more specific mark of the beast than that, inasmuch as on the one hand the vast majority of the papists (as they call us) do not wear one, while St. John testifies that all of the followers of the beast wear his mark, and, on the other hand, that those who do not wear the clerical crown will not be allowed to buy and sell, while, on the contrary, commerce is prohibited to those who wear it, this difficulty has thrown them into the interpretation that the mark of the beast must be invisible, which is itself a mark of their own beastly stubbornness.

Here, then, are many reasons to make and to receive the Sign of the Cross upon the forehead, both at Baptism and Confirmation and upon other occasions, in accordance with the practice of the Church of the Fathers. Thus St. Ambrose said, with reference to St. Agnes, that our Lord had marked her on her face so that she would receive no other suitors; and St. Augustine, commenting upon St. John, said that "Jesus Christ did not want the sign his faithful wore upon their foreheads to be a star, but his Cross, so that those who are thus humiliated will be glorified." And Victor Vitensis, describing the torture of a Christian by the Vandals, said that they had cut up his forehead so that it looked like a spider's web, "the forehead," he said, "upon which Jesus Christ had planted the standard of his Cross."

This custom meets with the complete disdain of the Evangelicals, while certain heretics in India, not content simply to make the Sign of the Cross at the baptism of their children, imprint it upon their foreheads with a hot iron. Fools are always to be found at the extremes.

Chapter 10

A Defense against Demons

If the holiness and authority of the Fathers have any weight with us, here are sufficient witnesses to the power of the Sign of the Cross.

St. Martial: "Keep always in your mind, in your mouth, and as a sign the Cross of the Lord in whom you have believed, true God and Son of God. For the Cross of the Lord is your invincible armor against Satan. It is a helm to defend your head, a breastplate to preserve your chest, a buckler to repel the arrows of the evil one, and a sword that will not allow the diabolical tricks and stratagems of the evil power to approach you. By this sign alone has heavenly victory been given to us, and by the Cross has baptism been sanctified."

St. Ignatius of Antioch, the disciple of St. John: "The prince of this world rejoices when someone renounces the Cross, for well does he know that the confession of the Cross is his defeat, inasmuch as it is the sign of the victory over his power: he is frightened to see it and fears to hear it."

Origen: "Let us rejoice, my beloved friends, and lift holy hands to heaven in the form of the Cross; when the demons see us armed in this way they will be crushed."

St. Athanasius: "Every magical art is rebuffed by the Sign of the Cross, and by it every spell is broken." And again: "Let him come forward, the one who wants to know about the pomp of demons, the trickery of the soothsayers, and the wonders of the magicians: let him make use of the Sign of the Cross—which the magicians will think absurd—merely naming Jesus Christ: he will see the demons chased off, the divinations cease, and all magic and spells destroyed."

Lactantius: "Just as Jesus Christ, when living among men, chased away demons by His word, so now His followers chase off the same evil spirits both by the name of their Master and by the sign of His Passion. This is not difficult to prove, for when sacrifices were made to demons, if someone present made the Sign of the Cross, the sacrifice was prevented."

St. Antony thus withstood the demons: "If you have any strength, if the Lord has given you any power over me, come, here I am, devour the one who is given to you. But if you cannot, why do you labor in vain? For the Sign of the Cross and faith in the Lord is an impregnable wall for us." And this is what Antony said to his disciples: "The demons come in the night pretending to be angels of God. Seeing them, arm yourselves and your homes with the Sign of the Cross, and immediately they will be reduced to nothing, for they fear this victory sign by which the Savior despoiled the powers of the air and made them laughable."

St. John Chrysostom: "St. Paul calls the Cross a prize [1 Cor. 7:23], and it should not only be made with the hand on the body, but, in truth, first in the soul. For if in this way you impress it upon your face, not one of the demons will dare to attack you, seeing the lance by which they received the mortal blow."

St. Ephraim: "Surround and adorn all your members with this life-giving sign, and evils will never approach you. For at the sight of this sign, the powers of evil take fright and flee."

St. Cyril of Jerusalem: "It is the sign of the faithful and the terrors of the demons, for the Lord triumphed over them with this sign. Show it forth boldly, for seeing the Cross they will remember the Crucifixion; they fear the one who crushed the head of the dragon."

St. Augustine: "If the enemy lies await in ambush, let the Christian know that with the word of the Creed and the Standard of the Cross he may march forward."

The Sign of the Cross

Thus we see the remarkable harmony of the voices of these irreproachable senators of the Church. Now let us consider some experiences that confirm what they have said.

One night while lying ill, St. Hilarion heard the crying of little children, the baaing of sheep, the lowing of cattle, and a cacophony of many different voices. When he understood that these were diabolical illusions, he knelt and signed his forehead with the Cross of Jesus Christ, so that thus armed with the helmet of faith, he could fight all the more valiantly. But as soon as he had invoked Jesus Christ, the whole apparition was swallowed up before his very eyes into a pit that suddenly opened up in the earth. The Cross fortified him, and—we should note—to make the Sign of the Cross is "to invoke Jesus Christ."

Lactantius related that some Christian servants who were attending their masters at a pagan sacrifice made the Sign of the Cross and thus chased off the demons so that the soothsaying could not take place. When the pagan priests understood what had happened, they caused the masters to become angry with the Christian religion and to cause countless injuries to the Church. Lactantius concluded his account with this argument against paganism: "The pagans said that their gods did not flee from the Cross because of fear, but because of hatred. Yes," replied Lactantius, "as if someone can hate another for any reason other than that the other can hurt him. If these gods had any majesty at all, they would torment and afflict those they hated rather than flee from them. Yet as they cannot approach those on whom they see the heavenly mark, nor injure those whom the immortal standard guards like an unassailable rampart, they are troubled and make their attack by means of the hands of others. Since they confess the truth of this fact, we are indeed the victors."

Truly this great man spoke well.

Julian the Apostate, wanting to know whether his attempt to become absolute master of the empire would succeed, followed a certain sorcerer and soothsayer into a deep grotto. During the descent he heard horrid noises, smelled a terrible stench, and saw flaming phantoms, "all of which frightened him terribly, so he had recourse to the Cross, with which he signed himself, taking for his protection the one He was persecuting." A marvelous occurrence: "The sign had power, the demons were overcome, and the noise ceased. What happened then? The evil man caught his breath and pressed onward newly steeled to his purpose; then the same frights came back all the stronger. Once again he had recourse to the Sign of the Cross, and the demons were silenced. Julian, an apprentice in these matters, was stupefied to see the demons defeated by the Cross. The master sorcerer reproved him, and, turning the event to his own advantage, said, 'This sign is an abomination to them, but they were not afraid of it.' The worse carried the day; Julian was persuaded." These are the words of St. Gregory Nazianzen, who, along with Theodoret, related the history.

St. Gregory the Great told us that a Jew, finding himself one night in a temple of Apollo where some demons were holding a council, signed himself with the Cross. The demons were unable to harm him. They said, "It is an empty vessel, but one that has been marked."

This is enough evidence for my purpose, but let us see what the author of the treatise will say to this, for he is always ready to speak.

To this last example he responds that "whoever wishes to draw a conclusion from this passage ought to say that these dialogues are full of frivolous tales." The foolish judge thus levies his sentence. It was St. Gregory the Great, the venerable Father, who told this tale. The author of the treatise, who is an unknown minister, accuses him of folly and lies: whom shall we believe? We would be in quite a fix if everything that is not to the taste of these innovators is to be held to be a fable. But what does he judge to be absurd in St. Gregory's testimony? Is it that demons meet in council? But Scripture expressly mentions such meetings (1 Kings 22:10–23; 2 Chron. 18:18–22), and St. John Cassian has provided a similar example. Is it that the Sign of the Cross stymies the efforts of the demons? But all of the oldest and purest Christians have believed and taught the same, and countless experiences support our belief. What, then, has incited my adversary to levy this judgment against St. Gregory, unless it is his rage to defend his own opinions?

Having thus responded to St. Gregory in particular, he gives these general arguments to dull the point of all of these alleged miracles and of others as well.

"God has often allowed things to be done of which He does not approve, as for instance the myriad miracles that once surrounded the pagan oracles. And when these things happen, as Moses says, speaking of the works wrought by false prophets [Deut. 13], God wants to test whether we fear and love Him alone. For it does not suffice to say that a marvelous thing occurred, but we must know that God is its author and whether the work tends to the glory of God and the salvation of men.

"In order to engrave upon the hearts of men a more profound understanding of the Passion and death of our Lord Jesus Christ in the early days of the preaching of the gospel, God willed that extraordinary things should sometimes happen. Nevertheless, if then it pleased God several times to show His generosity to His people, we must recognize it so as to thank Him for His help. But if He wished those who then saw little should see still less or even become blind, let us recognize His judgments and retain his truth in purity."

He continues: if these effects are thanks to "the power of Jesus Christ, then it is by means of the invocation of His name and not by a sign. If the effects are from an evil cause, the spell was chased off by a counter-spell, God allowing Satan to be able to do the work so that he might deceive men; the same Satan, seeing himself chased from his stronghold by Jesus Christ, has built another fortress against the same Jesus Christ by employing to that end the foolish simplicity of Christians, and in fleeing before the Cross he acts as one who retreats in order to advance."

Finally, speaking of the example of Julian the Apostate, he says that "the example of such a wretch should not be alleged to establish a doctrine of the Church, for such an example is not praiseworthy. In fact, the conclusion to draw from it is that since Julian the Apostate and others like him have made this sign and have, as they say, been aided, it is apparent that it does not proceed from God. Therefore it has come from Satan, who has sought to cause trouble with it, by the just judgment of God. Therefore this extraordinary occurrence served to confound this abominable man, both in his conscience as well as before God and man."

These are the arguments that my adversary has made, and now I shall oppose them.

First, they are full of contradictions and dubious claims. He does not know to whom the honor of these events should be given. "If it is by the power of Jesus Christ … if it is by the evil means … it could have happened so as to engrave upon their hearts a more profound conception of the Passion and death of Jesus Christ … it was because God gave Satan the power to deceive men." How embarrassing. Does not his irresolution show the poverty of his argumentation?

Second, antiquity as a whole stands against him with unparalleled agreement, by teaching that these marvels came from the hand of God. Would these great Fathers whom we have cited in such profusion have invited us to make the Sign of the Cross if they suspected that the Devil might be its author? And who will doubt that Jesus Christ was the true author, once he considers, as Lactantius pointed out, how much it tends to the honor of God that the mere sign of His Passion puts His enemies to flight?

The Sign of the Cross

Third, these arguments smell of heresy and desperation. It was the normal course for the rebels of old to attribute miracles to spells and the work of demons: witness the scribes and the Pharisees who attributed the works of Jesus Christ to Beelzebub (Matt. 12:24; Luke 11:15); the Vigilantians did the same to St. Jerome and the Arians to St. Ambrose. Here some words of Tertullian are worth noting. Persuading his wife that, if he were to die before her, she should not marry an infidel, he said, "Will you hide when you sign your bed and your body? Will it not seem that you are doing something magical?" Do you see that Tertullian attributed to the pagans the very thing that the Evangelicals say, that is, that the Sign of the Cross is a form of magic?

Fourth, the effect of such marvels has always been the glory of God and the salvation of men: all of the Fathers have said as much. Is it not to the glory of God and for the good of men when the Devil is cowed and rejected? To be sure, among the great effects of the Crucifixion of the Son of God should be included this one: "Now is the prince of this world cast out" (John 12:31). And this is why the demons flee from the Cross as though it were a living representation of the Crucifixion.

Fifth, inasmuch as the author of the treatise admits that it can be said that the miracles made by the Cross were accomplished by the power of God in order to engrave the thought of the Passion and death of our Savior upon the hearts of men, he has erred and shown himself to be unreasonable in seeking another cause of these miracles.

Sixth, his argument opens the door to the error that would interpret the miracles of exorcism done by our Lord and His disciples as the Devil retreating in order to advance. And as to what he says about the Devil working upon simple-minded Christians, there would be some semblance of truth to his argument if we were only able to adduce the testimony of idiots. But when men such as Ignatius, Origen, Chrysostom, and Augustine are led forth, how shall he dare to accuse them of a foolish simplicity or idiocy? Is there a man alive comparable to them either in ability or in holiness?

And as to the case of Julian the Apostate, the example of which my opponent says we ought not to follow, or rather, which he says should be rejected, I reply that it is a sign of his bad faith that he should be so unreasonable. For who has ever alleged that the example is significant because Julian the Apostate is the man in question? The example is significant because it shows that the Sign of the Cross has so much power against evil spirits that not only do they fear it in good hands, but also in the hands of whosoever makes it, and of this the case of Julian is clear proof. Truly, St. Gregory Nazianzen and Theodoret held resolutely that the demons fled for fear of the Cross. Allow us, sir, to follow their opinion rather than your own, or, worse, that of Julian's sorcerer. The soothsayer, as the Fathers explained, in order to avoid admitting that his masters the demons had fled in fear, told Julian that they held the Cross to be an abomination rather than a cause of fear. *Vincit quod deterius est*, said St. Gregory Nazianzen: the worse carried the day. But if, like my opponent, he had attributed the flight of the evil spirits to a ruse and stratagem, as if their object had been to pretend to flee so as to surprise the man all the more, then St. Gregory should have said *Vincit quod pessimum est*: the worst carried the day. And in truth, what reasonableness will be left in the world if it is permissible to interpret miracles this way? Would it not in the same way be possible to attribute even the resurrection of the dead to diabolical illusions?

But why would it have been necessary for the Devil to employ such tricks with Julian the Apostate or with the Jews about whom St. Gregory the Great wrote? What would have been the use of the subterfuge toward people who were already under his sway? How could he have acquired any additional power over Julian, who already worshipped him and was going into the grotto to pay him homage? Note, too, the word of St. Gregory Nazianzen, who said that Julian had recourse to the "old remedy," that is to say, to the Cross, the remedy he had learned when he was a Catholic. Ah, my adversary, you will one day have to give an account of these vain subtleties by which you twist all things according to your impiety.

No, your cleverness is stitched with the thinnest of threads, and the Devil has the better of you. How could it be from some stratagem that the Devil would flee the Cross? By this flight his own minions are led to defy his power, and good people are consoled, as have testified so many of the Fathers, who all reproach the evil one and those of his party for fleeing, while Julian was shaken by it and the Jew converted. But, says my adversary, Moses warned us not to believe in the marvels wrought by false prophets. All to the good, but the Cross is no false prophet; it is a holy sign, a sign of Christianity, as my opponent himself confesses, and the Devil fears him who makes it. So many saints have employed this sign in miraculous works: shall he dare to call them all false prophets?

Now, if from such miracles some have drawn superstitious conclusions, we must not therefore credit these miracles to the Devil. The marvels wrought by the bronze serpent were divine even though the people took them as an occasion for idolatry (2 Kings 18:4). We must, therefore, correct its abuse and restrain its use, as we not only do with good and holy things such as the Cross, but also with harmful and poisonous things. In the end, so many kinds of miracles other than putting demons to flight have been accomplished through the Sign of the Cross, miracles that cannot be ascribed to any trickery or stratagem of demons, which we ought not to believe it in this case either.

Chapter 11

The Power of the Sign of the Cross

The Cross has great power against the enemy for two reasons: the one is that it represents the death of the Savior, who abased and subjugated him, which this proud being hates and fears in the extreme; the other is that the Cross is a brief and powerful invocation of the Redeemer that can be employed on every occasion suitable for prayer. Now, can we think of an occasion in which prayer is not useful? To be a proof against poison, to restore sight to the blind, to heal the sick, to be a protection against our enemies: such are the uses of this holy sign.

Prochorus testified that St. John healed a man suffering from fever by making the Sign of the Cross and invoking the name of Jesus, and that the same saint marked the two legs of a lame man with the Sign of the Cross and commanded him to rise, and straightaway he did.

The story of the Arian bishop Cyrola and the blind man is justly famous. Having seen the Catholic bishops

The Sign of the Cross

Eugenius, Vindimialis, and Longinus work several miracles that strengthened the Catholic party, he thought that he could strike a great blow for his sect if he could do something that would make people believe that he had the same power. So he took a beggar and applied paste to his eyes so that he seemed to be blind and brought the beggar to the assembly to wait for him to pass by and to beg healing from him. This poor, manipulated man did as he was told and played the part. Cyrola tried to play his. He placed his hand upon this fake blind man and with certain words commanded him to open his eyes and see. Yet what happened was a true heretical miracle: the poor man who had pretended to be blind found himself truly to be, and with so sharp a pain in his eyes that it seemed to him that someone was plucking them out.

He accused himself of his trickery and his seducer as well, giving up the money he had received for this ploy, and he sought help and healing from the Catholic bishops. When they had heard him tell of his faith, they had pity upon him, "and seeking to defer to one another for the honor"—in the words of St. Gregory of Tours—"a holy dispute arose among them as to who would make the sign of the blessed Cross upon his eyes. Vindimialis and Longinus prayed Eugenius to do it; Eugenius for his part prayed them to impose their hands upon the man. This they agreed to do, while St. Eugenius made the Sign of the Cross over the eyes of the blind man, saying, 'In the name of the Father, and of the Son, and of the Holy Spirit, the true God, whom we confess Triune and equal in power: may your eyes be opened.' Immediately, the pain ceased and he was restored to health." Here, my dear adversary, you see the Sign of the Cross employed for the restoration of this poor wretch's sight, and the holy bishops wishing to defer to one another for the honor of doing it. Will you say that this was a trick of the Devil done in favor of the Catholics against the Arians? How shall you escape from this conundrum?

The Arians of Nicaea had obtained the church of the Catholics from the heretical emperor Valens. When St. Basil learned of it, he appealed to the emperor himself, so warmly upbraiding him for the wrong that he had done to the Catholics that the emperor at last put the matter into St. Basil's hands that he might resolve the difference, on the sole condition that he not allow himself to be moved by zeal for his own party in prejudice against the Arians. St. Basil accepted the charge and made this judgment — doubtless inspired by heaven — that the church should be shut up, sealed, and locked by both the Arians and the Catholics. Then, the Arians were to be given three days and three nights for prayer, after which they could come to the church and see whether it would open for them. If so, they would remain the owners forever. If not, then the Catholics would make their vigil for one night, after which they would come to the church, singing their psalms with the litany, and if it were to open for them, they would retain it in perpetuity, but if it were not to open, it would belong to the Arians. The Arians found this judgment acceptable, but the Catholics complained that it was too favorable to the Arians and that the heretics had been preferred out of fear for the emperor. Nevertheless, the sentence was carried out. The Arians prayed for three days and three nights, came to the doors of the Church (which had been extremely well secured, for each of the two parties had given it their best effort), and stayed there from sunrise until the hour of sext, crying out their *Kyrie eleisons*, but all for naught. In the end, tired of waiting, they departed.

Then St. Basil, calling together all the faithful, led them out of the city to the church of the martyr St. Diomede, where they spent the whole night in prayer. In the morning, he led them to the church, singing this verse: "Holy God, holy Mighty One, holy Immortal One, have mercy on us." Then, having arrived before the church where the Arians had been the day before, he said to the people: "Lift up your hands on high, to the Lord in heaven, and cry *Kyrie eleison*." While the people did this, St. Basil signed them and blessed them. Then he commanded them to be silent, and making the Sign of the Cross three times over the doors of the church, he said: "Blessed be the God of the Christians forever and ever. Amen." The people replied, "Amen," and by the power of their prayer the bolts and locks of the door fell off, and the doors flew open as if they had been pushed by a great wind. Then this great bishop sang: "O Princes, lift high your gates, rise up, you ancient doors, that the King of Glory may come in" (Ps. 23:7, 9). And entering into the holy temple with the people, he performed the divine mysteries.

O my dear adversary, if you have not yet been healed from having written your treatise, there are three or four points in this history that will be difficult for you to digest: churches dedicated to saints where the people go to pray to God; holy psalms chanted with litanies while processing; the episcopal blessing given to the people with the Sign of the Cross (*Sanctus episcopus illos consignans*, said St. Amphilochius, who is my source); and the Sign of the Cross used to work a miracle. Consider, too, the way that the text says that St. Basil entered the church to perform the divine mystery—*fecit divinum mysterium*: this is a phrase that cannot be reduced to prayer (they had, moreover, just spent the night in prayer), nor to a sermon, for preaching is not spoken of in this way, nor to be sure is your Lord's Supper, in which nothing divine is to be found but only the administration of bread that has already been prepared. I do not see how you will be able to respond to this testimony to the power of the Cross. For if you say that all this was the work of the Devil's cunning, St. Amphilochius will reply that by this miracle the Catholics were consoled and several Arians converted. What advantage can the Devil have gained from such an effect? And I reply that you are not sufficiently creditable to cast suspicion upon St. Basil for the use of magic or sorcery or upon St. Amphilochius for mendacity or subterfuge. If you say that St. Amphilochius attributed the miracle to the power of prayer, that is just what I want. For the Sign of the Cross is a part of the prayer made by St. Basil, both over the people when he blessed them and upon the doors themselves, and to what other end would he have made use of it?

A woman from Carthage had a sore upon her chest, an ailment that, according to the doctrine of Hippocrates, was entirely incurable. She sought the help of God, and, as the feast of Easter came near, she was told in a dream that she should go to the baptistery and have herself signed with the Cross by the first baptized woman that she met there. She did it and was immediately cured. My adversary is brought up short by this narrative. Having recounted the tale most impertinently, he then labors to strip it of its power. Here is how he tells the story: "A certain woman of Carthage was cured of a sore on her chest, having been told while sleeping to recognize by the Sign of the Cross the first baptized woman she would meet."

This is not true. She was not at all told to recognize the other woman by the Sign of the Cross, but to have this woman sign her by making the Sign of the Cross over the place where the sore was. The desire to win arguments carries away these poor Reformers. As to his interpretation, he gives it according to his custom, without any great candor, saying that this woman "had addressed herself to God alone," to whom — and not to any sign — she credited the healing. This is sheer madness. Whoever said that any healing or miracle, worked by the Sign of the Cross or in any other way, should be credited to anyone other than to God alone, who is the God of all consolation (2 Cor. 1:3)? Where he and I differ is on the question whether God employs the Sign of the Cross to work miracles through men, for it is beyond doubting that He often uses various things for supernatural effects. My adversary says no and does not understand why we say yes and prove it by experience. Is it not inept of him to say that it is God who works the miracle, inasmuch as no one is asking who did it, but how and by what instruments and means? It is God who cured her and could have cured her without sending her to the other woman who made the sign over her. Yet He did not wish to. Instead He sent her to the very means He wished to employ. Are we wiser than He? Shall we say that His means were ill-chosen? If it please Him that we so employ them, shall we then reject them?

Now it is St. Augustine who was the author of this history, and he judged this marvel so fitting a subject for the praise of God that he scolded the woman for not having sufficiently publicized the miracle. A good Evangelical, to the contrary, would bury it away, from zeal for the purity of the Reform. But the great souls of old were content with the purity of the original form.

After all, the prayer that is the Sign of the Cross was held in such high esteem in the ancient and primitive Church that it was in constant use. It was employed as a general preservative from evil, both at sea and on land, as St. John Chrysostom has told us, to cure animals of their illnesses and people of possession. St. Martin used it to divide the enemy troops and pass through their midst, for he was armed with the Sign of the Cross, as Sulpicius Severus tells us. St. Lawrence used it to heal the blind. The dying Paula signed her mouth with the Cross. The martyr St. Gordius went joyfully to his torture in Caesarea because he was forearmed with the Sign of the Cross, as St. Basil recounted. The great St. Antony, encountering that woodland monster — some sort of faun or centaur — as he went to see St. Paul the Hermit, immediately made the Sign of the Cross to protect himself. And I cannot forget the book of Mathias Flaccus Illyricus, published with additions in Geneva itself, the one called *A Catalogue of Witnesses to the Truth*, which by an extraordinary impudence cites St. Antony against us, saying that he could not discover that the saint had ever made the Sign of the Cross. For how long shall the people be misled? Truly, the testimony I produced in the previous chapter was taken from St. Athanasius, and this one is from St. Jerome.

Now, I have said that in these events the Cross shows itself to have the power of a most efficacious prayer, from which it follows that things that have been signed have a particular holiness, as having been blessed and sanctified by this holy sign and by this celebrated prayer, which is full of power because it was instituted, approved, and confirmed by Jesus Christ and by the whole of his Church.

Biographical Note

St. Francis de Sales

(1567-1622)

Doctor of the Church and patron saint of writers, St. Francis de Sales was remarkable "not only for the sublime holiness of life which he achieved, but also for the wisdom with which he directed souls in the ways of sanctity."[9]

The eldest of thirteen children, Francis de Sales was born in 1567 to a noble family in the French-speaking Duchy of Savoy (an area straddling present-day eastern France and western Switzerland). He received a superb education in both France and Italy. Although intended by his father for a diplomatic career, St. Francis was ordained to the priesthood in the diocese of Geneva in 1593. Shortly thereafter, he was sent to the Chablais region of the Savoy on a mission to persuade those who had fallen under Calvinist influence to return to the practice

[9] Pope Pius XI, *Rerum omnium perturbationem*, 4.

of Catholicism. St. Francis spent four years laboring at this difficult task, during which he suffered many indignities. More than once he was thrown out of his lodgings and had to sleep in the open air. Many times he celebrated Mass in empty churches or continued preaching while the congregation walked out. Nevertheless, St. Francis's unflagging poise and kindness in this mission led to its eventual success. By the turn of the century, the majority of the area's inhabitants had returned to the Catholic faith.[10]

After his election as bishop of Geneva in 1602, St. Francis continued his apostolic efforts to win souls back to the Catholic Church. At the same time, he sought to build a broad community of devout persons within the Church who would live the life of Christian perfection in all their varied states and vocations.[11]

It was St. Francis's absolute conviction that "holiness is perfectly possible in every state and condition of secular life," whether one is male or female, rich or poor, single or married.[12] He expounded this view at length in his classic

[10]Pope Pius XI, *Rerum omnium perturbationem*, 8.
[11]Francis de Sales, *Jane de Chantal: Letters of Spiritual Direction*, eds. Wendy M. Wright and Joseph F. Power (New York: Paulist Press, 1988), 23.
[12]Pius XI, *Rerum omnium perturbationem*, 13.

work *Introduction to the Devout Life*. This conviction permeates the advice he gave to the many persons from all walks of life to whom he gave spiritual direction, both in person and in letters renowned for their spiritual wisdom, their psychological insight, their graciousness, and what one scholar has called their "inspired common sense."[13]

Jane Frances Frémyot, Baroness de Chantal, is the most famous of those who came to St. Francis for spiritual direction. An aristocratic young widow with four children, she met St. Francis in 1604. In cooperation with her, St. Francis founded the Visitation of Holy Mary in Annecy in Savoy, a congregation for unmarried and widowed women who aspired to religious life but who were not sufficiently young, healthy, or free of family ties to enter one of the more austere women's orders of the day.

The Visitation eventually developed into a cloistered religious order devoted to prayer and the cultivation of the "little virtues" St. Francis praised so highly. The order flourished during St. Francis's lifetime and afterward. St. Jane de Chantal was herself canonized in 1751.

After nearly thirty years of tireless labor on behalf of the Church and her members, St. Francis de Sales died of

[13]Elisabeth Stopp, ed., *St. Francis de Sales: Selected Letters* (New York: Harper and Bros., 1960), 33–34.

a cerebral hemorrhage in Lyons, France, on December 28, 1622. He had been traveling in the entourage of the king and queen of France at the time, but rather than stay in royal quarters, he lodged in the gardener's cottage on the grounds of the Visitation convent in that city. Fittingly for this apostle of the little virtues, he died in that modest cottage.

St. Francis de Sales was canonized in 1665. His feast day is celebrated on January 24.

The preceding biographical note, written by the staff of Sophia Institute Press, was originally published in St. Francis de Sales's *Thy Will Be Done* (Sophia Institute Press, 1995).

Other books from Sophia Institute Press
by St. Francis de Sales:

Thy Will Be Done
The Art of Loving God
Finding God's Will for You

Sophia Institute

Sophia Institute is a nonprofit institution that seeks to nurture the spiritual, moral, and cultural life of souls and to spread the Gospel of Christ in conformity with the authentic teachings of the Roman Catholic Church.

Sophia Institute Press fulfills this mission by offering translations, reprints, and new publications that afford readers a rich source of the enduring wisdom of mankind.

Sophia Institute also operates two popular online Catholic resources: CrisisMagazine.com and CatholicExchange.com.

Crisis Magazine provides insightful cultural analysis that arms readers with the arguments necessary for navigating the ideological and theological minefields of the day. *Catholic Exchange* provides world news from a Catholic perspective as well as daily devotionals and articles that will help you to grow in holiness and live a life consistent with the teachings of the Church.

In 2013, Sophia Institute launched Sophia Institute for Teachers to renew and rebuild Catholic culture through service to Catholic education. With the goal of nurturing the spiritual, moral, and cultural life of souls, and an abiding respect for the role and work of teachers, we strive to provide materials and programs that are at once enlightening to the mind and ennobling to the heart; faithful and complete, as well as useful and practical.

Sophia Institute gratefully recognizes the Solidarity Association for preserving and encouraging the growth of our apostolate over the course of many years. Without their generous and timely support, this book would not be in your hands.

www.SophiaInstitute.com
www.CatholicExchange.com
www.CrisisMagazine.com
www.SophiaInstituteforTeachers.org

Sophia Institute Press® is a registered trademark of Sophia Institute.
Sophia Institute is a tax-exempt institution as defined by the
Internal Revenue Code, Section 501(c)(3). Tax I.D. 22-2548708.